The Great Road Travel Book

The guide to journeying the world by road

By Lennie Hardingham

Contents

Introduction

Chapter 1

What is overlanding

- Travelling off-the-cuff
- Self-reliance
- Memories
- Personal achievement
- The different forms of overlanding
- Working
- Hire a car
- Tours

Chapter 2

Who goes overlanding

- The simple answer
- Why
- Men and Women
- Time
- The hard routes
- Easy routes
- The dangers and insanity
- Solo
- Teams
- The inspiration

Chapter 3

Preparing

- The 5 p's
- Creating a well-balanced team
- Make it a team effort
- Time x2
- Budget
- Keep your money safe
- Routes
- All is lost
- Smell the roses
- Maps
- Check the news
- Guide books
- Your vehicle
- Choosing your vehicle
- Maintenance

- Tools
- Vehicle Documents
- Fiche forms
- Know your vehicle
- Accommodation
- Basic camping skills
- Food
- What are your essentials
- Possible Overland food list
- Overland equipment Checklist
- Clothing
- Vaccinations
- Events
- Weather
- 12 months To Do list
- Passports
- Visas
- Carrying luggage
- Health and fitness

Chapter 4

Fundraising

- Fundraising for your event
- Saving
- Event
- Putting out a plea
- Sponsors
- Small business sponsors
- Corporate sponsors
- Charities
- Persistence

Chapter 5

Survival driving

- Overland survival driving
- Using your gears correctly
- Snow and Ice
- Mud and Sand
- Acceleration
- Breaking
- Coasting
- Steering
- Maintenance
- Getting stuck
- Winches

Chapter 6

Surviving continents

- Food
- Cooking
- Shopping
- Wildlife
- Wildlife and food
- Camping
- Hotels and hostels
- Changing your route
- Safety
- Money
- Fires
- Insects
- Toilets
- Do everything
- Smell the roses
- Inspiration

- Moral boosting during

- How to influence others to get what you want

- Keep an open mind

Introduction

Within the contents of this book is the intent to inspire and excite you to pursue a dream of driving around the world and have incredible adventures and experiences. To many this is called overland travel. Here in this book, I share knowledge that I have acquired over 30 years of the most in-depth form of travel. You will be given the tools to help you create, plan, and live a successful expedition.

If you are an adventurist at heart or secret wannabe adventure traveller, through these pages, you will be introduced to the courageous, outgoing, and confident adventurer that is within you. Your imagination will be stretched, and you will know more about the journey you desire and why you must persist in pursuit of it.

This book offers you the principles to create not only an adventure that will prepare you and your mind for the experience of your life, but to use in everyday events that will happen throughout your existence on earth.

You will gain an outlook to overlanding that is rarely seen, however in order to experience your adventure in the most fulfilling way for your mind and future appetite for living and travelling, you should consume all the material of this book, as it will enhance your ability as an overlander and will give you the impetus to explore and acquire the faith in yourself and the will and persistence to fulfil your dreams that will know no bounds.

Highlight the parts of this book that interest you the most as you go along and once you have finished reading it, go back and read over the highlighted sections until you have fully absorbed the content.

Chapter 1

What is overland travel

"If a small and tenuous population of proto-humans had not survived a hundred slings and arrows of outrageous fortune (and potential extinction) on the savannas of Africa, then Homo sapiens would never have emerged to spread throughout the globe".

Stephen Jay Gould

For over well over 200,000 years humankind has been evolving into the most curiosity filled creature to have ever explored the earth. Our lust for greener pastures and to be the first, has fuelled our heart and souls for adventure.

It's no surprise then, that the adventure tourism trade has grown to be a multibillion-dollar enterprise. To this day and more than ever before, our over whelming passion pushes us to further our ability and to push ourselves to more daring limits. It is what took us out of the jungle and into space. There basically is not anything that we would not try.

At present there is plenty of scientific evidence that shows why our ancestors started spreading out globally and in a lot of cases concerned our unique association with the animal world. As food sources changed and became more diverse so to our, habits and locations changed as we began to evolve our lust for faraway lands, where we began to develop our innate curiosity for the unknown.

Travelling off the cuff with limited detailed plans and truly going into the unknown, is not only exciting, but also invigorating, its character building and confidence growing, and it can be very much life changing.

I have always had a growing and burning desire to share my experiences with others and to inspire fellow adventurers and life fulfillers like yourself and show that there is more to overland travel than having your hand held by a guide. Adventure travel now makes up around 26 to 30% of tourism and people are always looking for new and exciting ways to get around the globe. We want to see more, do more and live more. We want to have experiences that will last our lifetime, we want stories to tell the next generations.

In a land where health and safety are all-powerful, and a daredevil wants to be unleashed, we want to know what we can do different and how we can do it.

Suit you, Sir

So, what venture would most suit you? This would of course depend entirely on the individual and what it is that you want out of your unique experience. Think of it as a tailored suit that has been made exclusively for you by a master tailor and like the suit your adventure will be made to measure to fit your own personal wants, needs and ambitions.

There are tailor-made adventure tours that are designed to fit around loose budgets, as there will be plenty of extras such as excursions that will tempt the hardiest of penny pinchers. They offer plenty of variety that will give a large group of tourists many great experiences, but you can't please all of the people all of the time.

Up and coming adventure

A growing phenomenon that explores our passion for adventure is overland travel.

This is a relatively new form of seeing the world and it isn't just appealing to the hardened traveller, it is also finding its way into the imagination of the more common traveller. Who has wanted to take more chances in life, but usually makes the excuse of the risk being too great or having no time due to circumstances in their life.

Overland travel or overlanding is travelling by roads, tracks and in particular and what this book is focused on, making your own path up to remote destinations around the world by driving your own vehicle or that you have use of.

This book isn't just about getting the most out of a modern-day cross country driving adventure, it has been written to inspire you to take the leap of faith and go and to explore, conquer and create your own history.

Overlanding is a way to go into the deepest part of the country's culture and to experience life from their perspective.

It gives you the opportunity to find out what is down that road or over that hill at relatively little effort, time or expense.

On more than one occasion during my early days of travelling, which was mostly with all my belongings stuffed into an old rucksack where it seemed that whatever I was looking for was always way down the bottom, I would be using public transport. Which was unreliable to say the least.

Being sardined into an overcrowded sweat box was starting to lose its appeal.

You will always be just looking through the window at places that might hold some interest as the driver approaches a bend on the wrong side of the road whilst being stressed by his over burdened wife, instead of having the ability to stop when you want and take a leisurely look around.

Self-reliance and freedom of overlanding

The freedom of choice and to go to the small town you passed 10 miles back and just being able to stop for refreshments without your hair turning grey is very satisfying and gives a pleasing sense of freedom.

Being able to drive at your own speed and take a different route that you've discovered is a scenic bypass through a mystic valley are all things that turn a trip into an adventure.

Our basic human needs

Driving a vehicle with its best days behind it, across Mountain ranges, deserts, Jungles, hostile towns and cities and vast continents would almost certainly fulfil most of our human needs. Such as, to be in control of the situation or certainty of a situation, which is a survival instinct to keep us from harm, or to gain pleasure in doing something we know we will enjoy.

Another need is having variety or uncertainty, it excites, thrills, and fills you with curiosity and it is why we explore and venture out and grow as a race.

Also, the feeling of importance or significance. Feeling special, needed, or unique is a fundamental need that we all have buried deep within us. Some people like to feel important by bullying or making threats. Others may feel the need to smile and help wherever possible.

Let me say to you that making someone feel special and important is the best way to get them on your side, extremely handy to know when your being held at a difficult border crossing in the middle of nowhere.

One of the most important needs and one you will certainly achieve on your travels is the need to grow. Everything in life must grow to serve a purpose. If it doesn't have a purpose, it simply withers away and dies.

The independence of over landing will grow and enhance you in more ways than just becoming a better driver.

One example is that you will become more resourceful and inventive, as when your vehicle breaks down, let's just say where you really don't won't it to. The creative part of your brain will go into overdrive. You will get better and more resourceful at finding ways out of the toughest situations and back on the road as quickly as possible.

Eventually this will stand you in better stead each time it happens.

Another need is the need to contribute. Whether it is having a sponsored charity adventure or simply to share your knowledge on your return from your journey, because you will not be able to help yourself you must and will share and contribute people's ears off.

Many people love the idea of driving across unknown and distant lands. It is the romance of the experience and seeing only what they have ever imagined.

I speak through experience when I say that once you have survived and lived to tell the tale of your first overland adventure, there will be no stopping you in getting that feeling back. And your second one must be even more remote, longer and more daring than the last.

An overland adventure is not your normal 'Stay in the hotel' type holiday, drinking cocktails by the sea and laying on the beach until you are London bus red.

They are adventures that require you to think and act! They need to be planned and nurtured with a growing sense of excitement.

This will surpass your imagination to heights you have never felt before. You will feel you have the enthusiasm to go and do everything you have always dreamt of all at once.

Memories

Personally, I am not a great fan of the tourist in sandals and long socks, with the floppy hat and a camera with a lens that would feel at home amongst the giant redwoods, whilst snapping 50 pictures of the same thing.

But I do believe in taking pictures that give a lasting memory, although I think 2 or 3 is sufficient. After which the rest should be for you and only you to reflect upon, as and when you feel.

Looking back through your photo albums you will relive the epic times you experienced which in turn gives you the sense of achievement you had, way back then.

These memories last a lifetime and never leave you.

They will always give you a connection to the person or persons with whom you travelled whilst making lifelong friends and special bonds.

Personal achievement

Over the years I have worked for overland companies and drove independently on many occasions, and each time I finished a particularly challenging route I felt an overwhelming sense of achievement.

When I drive the first few feet, I feel grateful for being given the opportunity of being able to do this and to the other members in my team for the journey we are about to embark on and the experiences we will share.

It has taken a lot of planning and demanding work to get here and realise then that it has all been worth it.

Along the route I see the amazing sights for which I have longed. I see and share cultures with locals. Feel the different climates and altitudes and what nature has blessed our planet with.

Every time I look around me, I feel honoured and successful. A sense of attainment that will keep me going through to the end.

Whatever vehicle you take will be put to the test and will have a good chance of breaking down. Yes, you can do as much as you can to reduce the chance of breaking down, but some of the roads in less developed countries are car killers and do their best to shake every part loose from its anchor. But all said and done when you finally get your beloved vehicle to its final destination, because beloved it will become, you will feel the overwhelming sense of pride and triumph you deserve.

You and your team, of whatever size, will know that you have pulled each other through and accomplished what you set out do.

The different forms of over landing

On quite a few occasions during an expedition, I have met other people travelling cross country in their own way. What I mean by this that they may be driving a 4x4, camper conversion or an RV (recreation vehicle).

Everyone has their own preference and choice of travel. In an RV or camper, you have a lot of the necessities and comforts of home. Saves time and inconvenience. You can also get them in all wheel drive form with ruggedness and strength to take on most places. There are the draw backs of expense. But if you can afford it, it's a good way to go, but remember they will often be heavier and larger, which could cause some problems in many cities and certain road or off-road surfaces, where a shorter wheelbase offers much more flexibility when going off road and on difficult surfaces.

RV's and campers come equipped with full kitchen facilities and most of the time toilets and showers. Which can be a total blessing after a long hike or strenuous activity.

However, it does mean looking for somewhere to empty the toilet and fill up with water. Not the most romantic of jobs but we do what we need to do to have the time of our lives.

Whilst travelling through the United States where it is compulsory to use a campground, you could find RV sites everywhere.

A few occasions the sites were pleasant and lots of space for an RV, but the majority of the time the spaces were cramped and impersonal.

Camping on the European continent is similar in many respects, although you could get away with more roadside overnight parking which would be cheaper but lack the facilities.

I am fortunate enough to have experienced different forms of overland travel. I have no real favourite and enjoyed and gained through them all and as long as you are planning ahead with a resourceful attitude, then not much will stop you

I have taken a Suzuki jeep through Africa. Brilliant for off roading, and although the one litre engine was good at low speeds and despite it still being able to pull over steep inclines it was up against it on tarmac or highways. That little engine kept cooking and had two new head gaskets and untold spare parts fitted to keep it alive. It broke down at least thirty times, but with a stubborn resilience my teammate and I got it to its destination.

Taking a van can be a particularly good idea and make a lot of sense.

It is always going to be sufficient in size and space. They have a stronger suspension and considering they are built to carry a load heavier than what you will use it for, it should last longer and with that in mind they also have an engine and gearbox with extra strength and torque that could be a god send. However, vans before turbo's were known for being sluggish and embarrassing as they tried to climb a steep speed bump, with only a heavy bag of shopping on-board. So, a good turbo is a must.

You could also use it to sleep in on occasions if you could not camp or find an hotel. Making it more an ideal vehicle to consider.

Overlanding for your job

You could if you were determined enough get a job with a tour company who take passengers around in a truck designed for over landing or, so they say.

There are two options here, first you could be a tour leader which would involve you in the day to day running of the entire tour, keeping all passengers happy, which is an impossible task at best. Tour leaders are usually stressed and under pressure, if that is you and you like a lot of pressure in your life and often feel the need to tear your own hair out, then this is a good option for.

If you are like me, you could become a driver. You get to drive a truck across great continents. You're required to not just drive, but maintain the truck to a good standard, keep it clean and to drive it as comfortably as possible.

If needed, you should be able to help the passengers and tour leader where ever you can and this could be anytime of the day or night. In return you get to see some amazing sights and go on excursions with your passengers. You get free accommodation and food or food allowance sometimes.

This role does however require you to be very resourceful and truck savvy as you will have very worried tourist relying on you to get them to safety and not leave them stranded on top of a mountain pass.

I have fixed punctures and burst hydraulic pipes at above 5000 metres before now, where any help is two or three days away.

The pay is extremely poor, but the experience and lifestyle are worth the low pay.

Hire a car

On a recent visit to the United States, travelling from Boston to San Francisco myself and a friend drove over 13,000 miles seeing and doing as much as our heads and wallets could take over 3 months.

We planned our trip well, but changed our minds on the RV route as we had a budget we were determined to stick to.

As we looked for a cheaper option, we discovered hiring a car was the way to go. We got a good standard of car with a big trunk and off we went, simple!

A couple of nights in an hotel already burnt a hole in our wallets.

So, it was up to Wal-Mart for a new tent and gazebo.

Always buy a tent that is twice what it says it is. i.e.: if described as a 2-man tent, then get a 4-man tent. Four men get an 8 man. This will give you much needed space on hot sticky nights and make it feel more comfortable.

The gazebo, which if possible, acquiring one with a fly net, can give you that feeling of extra space and protect you from rain. It will help protect you whilst you cook or simply playing cards outside your tent.

A car will allow you to go to more difficult places and is much more manoeuvrable around cities and parking at stores or hotels.

They are much cheaper to hire and cheaper to run than a big 4X4, van or RV.

However, cars not being as big as vans, you will certainly be stacking everything on top of each other.

But if that is your only problem you could always add a small box trailer to your collection.

4X4 or not 4X4

Well that really does depend on what you like, where you're going and when you are going there.

If you like a bit more space and don't mind the sometimes-cumbersome agility of 4X4's, then you should consider hiring or buying one.

Virtually all road journeys in this day and age are on tarmac of average standard, so I would just say get a car.

The roads that I experienced in Mauritania, west Africa were either dust, sand, mud or paved, which means it had some paving around the creator sized holes that were barely passable.

In fact, the constant avoiding of these holes would have been much more of an effort in a 4X4.

There are some really good four-wheel drive cars now a days, with a shorter wheelbase for that agility. A long wheelbase will of course offer you more in the terms of space and the convenience of not having to unload the trunk each time you wanted a change of underwear.

I love driving off road vehicles and would usually choose one if the money is right or it was necessary that I needed one. But it would have to be able to change into two wheeled drive to save fuel and less work on the engine.

26

The electric revolution

One year before covid I was asked if I would like to lead an expedition. It would take a team of four up the spine of South America, an area with which I am well acquitted. However, it came with a twist, and that twist was going to be revolutionary and rule breaking. Attempting it would take planning on a military scale.

There would certainly be hardships and daily challenges that would make a crocodile cry. So, I jumped at the chance.

Electric vehicles have one major design fault for a quest like this. Where the bloody hell do we plug it in. Now I'm no scientist, but I can still work out that carrying a trailer load of potatoes to charge a battery of a 2-ton 4x4 is not very practical. As for solar panels, unless the roof is the size of an aircraft carrier, we were going to need to think this one through.

I have said in this book, "there is always a way". Planning a route through small towns and villages would help us on many parts, which is until our heavy vehicle put to much of a strain on their unreliable electricity source. Then there is the vastness of the South American continent. Towns and villages will be days apart and civilisation can be parse.

It seemed that for these parts' long breaks and plenty of rations, many forms of entertainment and a shit load of patients would be needed, as we use large, the more powerful the better solar panels to charge the batteries. Of course, with environmental issues within this quest a generator could not be used, nor hybrid vehicles, just in case that was what you were thinking.

There would also be other ways, such as wind generation. Much of the time we would be in mountainous or coastal areas, and hooking portable mini turbines could give use a helpful boost. This planning was to be in vain for the moment at least.

Lockdown kept our spirits down for a while but our passion for adventure keeps rising. C'est la vie. That is how it goes sometimes on the road. But there is always a way, and more opportunities will come.

More on Vehicles in chapter 3

Tour companies

If you are looking for an easy option, I would recommend using a tour company. All you will have to do is pay the money and get any visa's you might need.

The tour company will pretty much do the rest.

Just take your imagination, your passport, your backpack and credit card and you are set for the time of your life.

You are required to follow sets of rules such as time keeping, cleanliness, no drink and drugs on the vehicle and payments of excursions. You also need to try and be respectful of the other passengers as when strangers start to become familiar with other people's traits and habits that begin to find them annoying, then tensions can flare up.

You are very much free to enjoy yourself and do what you like and get the tour leader to do nearly everything for you. But like the rest of the passengers, you may be upset when the tour leader has forgotten something you required because you were sixth in line of a request that was given to them whilst they are sorting out the roster for the next three days.

The downside to any tour is the sheep factor. You may have to attend group meetings, go on organised tours or even to the restaurant. Although it is not completely compulsory to follow the group on these events, you may feel you have to or be looked upon as an outcast. This is the 'off the peg' version of the suit and caters for the many rather than the one.

You can only go on the route specified on the days itinerary and only stop if the driver wants to stop, of course, time permitting. But sometimes if you can whisper a friendly word in the driver's ears, he may stop at an attraction for you or to let you off for a very quick pit stop to relieve yourself at a nearby tree or bush.

Chapter 2

"Overland travel is doing what only a few have done, those who seek to grow, the brave, the passionate, the leaders, those with faith and a burning desire and those who ask a question of themselves and get an answer they weren't expecting".

-The Author

Who goes overlanding

Simple answer

Based on my own experiences and those with whom I have travelled with, the simple answer is that 'anyone' could embark on a great adventure; However, the reality can be slightly more complex.

Most people I know back in my hometown would say to me they would love to do what I have done but given the opportunity just how many of them would take it up and do what they speak. Going on an average of one hundred people ten would say right that is it I'm doing it. But only one would actually follow through with their dream.

If you are reading this right now and are making positive plans that you can't back out from, congratulations, you are in a minority of people who against all odds and procrastinations are living their lives and overcoming your fears.

Those of you who only dream and do not travel, regardless of having the opportunity, are the ones who make the excuses of not putting the effort in to fulfil an ambition. The fear of losing their jobs and stepping out of comfort zones have become so familiar.

In reality it is not really that difficult to go on a tour and do something out of the ordinary.

It is not really the money they are worried about but the fact they are going into the unknown and through countries that are known to them for having a bad reputation, just because that is what they have heard.

When the adventurer comes to the surface and you have made up your mind and nothing will deter you from this opportunity to broaden your horizons, you must put all else on hold and begin your quest to glory.

It is not always straight forward nor logical, and emergencies always seem to crop up when you least expect or need them, but whatever is more important at that time, get it done and out of the way and if so without missing a day of planning, if possible, because if one day is missed then it becomes much easier to start missing more and the negative thoughts will start creeping in and so will the excuses.

Why?

People in general have gone on an adventure because they want excitement in their lives. Excitement is the definition of happiness. When you are excited about something you are happy. When you travel there is an outcome and excitement of achieving that outcome.

Sometimes people will give up their jobs and even change their lives to have this outcome and most of the time they are right, because upon their return they are filled with more confidence and belief and want to carry this into a new way of living and thinking.

I can guarantee that a traveller's state of mind will be fundamentally different to what it was before they embarked on their great journey. There is no tangible way to say what the average overlander does for a living as I have travelled with truck drivers, web designers, corporate managers, nuclear welders and the list goes on.

But they all had one thing common they all wanted excitement and great experiences. So much so, that

33

would put their lives from their rat race normality on hold and risk going into an unknown adventure to find it.

The average age for this type of travel can vary from 18 to 80. Although the majority are 28 to 45 which is still a large age gap.

This all makes for a good combination of people wanting to see the world.

You would be very unlucky if on your travels you didn't come across someone who is doing similar to yourself.

The variety of adventure with overland travel will always shape into a good story and lead to sometimes gasping conversations.

Men and Women

It is a time for change on our planet and to see different points of view. Long have the days gone when it was the man who was the sole bread winner.

Rights and equality are the big thing, and it shows absolutely everywhere.

Having a more equal outlook certainly makes for better opportunities and a much-varied selection of adventurers. This is great news for everyone who wants to be and who already is an overland adventurer.

It has been men who have dominated the adventure travel lifestyle for so many years. But the past 20 or so years it has had a change for the better and the number of women who are facing their fears have soared to great heights. Giving a new lease of life and different perspectives to seeing the world.

Women have a fear of travelling through dangerous countries where they are considered the inferior sex, but some do it anyway.

These are the 1% of those who would have no hesitation to live their life the way they want to and to face their fears, despite what they have heard from others. There are plenty of options for women to travel, these include overland tour companies, who offer a safer approach to living an adventure as group travel keeps growing.

Not all men are inspired to take a leap of faith and face their fears with adventure travel, but those who do are more willing to chance much more than the usual stay in bed Steves. They like the women want to build up a log of experiences and see as much as they can. But remember quality is always better than quantity. You can see everything and learn somethings, but you need to learn from less and experience it to gain wisdom.

Time

When it comes to managing time and living your dream by doing something that gives you the sense of achievement that you so definitely want and need, you must in turn be flexible and willing to compromise.

Start with a few days of travelling if you must, then do 2 or 3 weeks driving from London to Gambia for example is a great start and would be very rewarding and life changing in some cases.

The more and longer you do the more you let your imagination run wild and free.

The digital age is here for the foreseeable future and continues to grow and grow. If you are not online, you pretty much don't exist.

Worrying about it is not going to make it better but embracing it and making it work for you could be highly beneficial and make the planning of your trip far easier. Planning time is much easier with so called maps giving ETA's and itineraries. All of which can be organised in spreadsheets.

I have been on expeditions where the last two weeks have had to be rushed as two of the team had to get back to their jobs.

The rest of the team lost out on doing a huge chunk of route that was planned. But regardless we were still a team and got them to the destination on time and safely.

If you are in employment makes sure you always give yourself at least 3 days leeway and time to reflect and settle upon your return home. This will be a great asset to your teammates and yourself.

Eventually over the years you will know how to master your time to fit in with your travel plans. Planning is always key to success, but remember, plans are made to be broken. You will find more on time in the next chapter.

Hard routes

Overland expeditions can be put into 2 different categories.

Tough and Easy or Hard and Soft.

Each one can bring happiness and fulfilment to the participant.

But if you take the one that isn't for you, you may find climbing an active volcano to difficult or a wine tasting tour uninspiring. You might have booked yourself onto a group travel tour and realise early on that it is definitely not for you.

It could also work the other way, whereupon you decided to travel in a vehicle of your own and hate every minute.

This all should come into play during your planning. No one knows you better than you and you need to take a step back and look at yourself and then pile on the questions.

What type of person am I?

Do I get lonely?

Do I like to socialise and like the company of different people?

Am I a control freak and would that annoy others?

Do other people's annoying habits annoy me?

How resourceful am I?

How much do I like nature?

Is this type of travel for me?

There are many more questions to ask yourself to help judge what you really want and how it can be for you.

Whatever type you choose there will be some element of stress along the line. You will have difficult days and so will your team.

That is just how it is. But you can reduce your participation in it by trying to keep calm and keeping an open mind. See it from their point of view.

Hard routes would be travelling through south America or other places with similar terrain. Where you may get your vehicle stuck on a regular basis or break down in the middle of a desert or high mountain pass.

You may be camping in areas that are thick wilderness and require you to dig your own latrine, sometimes that could be a more favourable option than some of the hotels you will come across.

It really can be a hardship when you get your vehicle stuck or stranded.

You may even breakdown as I did in Rabat the capital of Morocco with a torn head casket. But because we persevered, we found locals to help us. Although a day and a half late we had a perfectly running car that would eventually take us to where we wanted to be with a lot more gratitude and relief.

Hard routes can take you through some of the most hostile places on earth.

Personally, I have almost never had any trouble not to say you will not.

But still, you must go there with the right attitude. Be friendly and sincere.

Smile, make friends and offer gratitude.

Most of time the locals want to be intrigued by your story.

Easy routes

The second category "soft" is not always the choice of words which you associate with overlanding.

But there are ways to even cater for the most home comfort lovers to have ever possessed a passport.

Driving your own or rented car across Europe and north America and staying on the tarmac until you reach your hotel would be considered as being a soft form of travelling.

I have on a few occasions hired a car to drive across the United States and Europe, and my personal choice is camping, but it's not for everyone.

When you hire a car, you have a bit of hassle at the start when you have to collect the vehicle but after that it's plain sailing.

There is no real worry about break downs because you know it will be fixed or replaced. The insurance and taxes are all part of the agreement, and they are usually new and low mileage, which is very reassuring.

Making for a lot less worry and minimal aggravation.

Going on tours and becoming part of a tour group is definitely one way to consider if you are looking for the easiest way through.

The Biggest overland companies running the largest number of trucks are:

Tucan travel

They have the big yellow trucks to advertise themselves as a good class adventure tour company. You will get a driver and a tour leader. They can be a bit slow to respond to your questions but will do their best.

They don't treat their staff great and have a high turnover. In my experience if you have happy staff, you have thrilled customers. However, they do employ experienced drivers with a mechanical background.

Dragoman

Much smaller trucks than Tucan and older but have the ability to go off the beaten track a little more, as they put it. Their staff go through 6 weeks training in UK before they leave on a tour. They are slightly cheaper but because of the in-house training, most of the drivers have only just passed their heavy goods licenses and then are expected to go to south America.

Oasis travel

The smaller of the 3 and with a little more soul. They run very much like Tucan just with a bit more care.

They send new tour drivers who have experience in heavy goods out for a few months on tours with more experienced tour drivers.

These companies all do roughly the same routes, but prices do vary and so do attitudes.

Dangers

Einstein once said in that famous quote: *"The definition of insanity was doing the same things over and over again and expecting a different result."*

One of the biggest questions you will come across from people you talk to about your upcoming adventure is the danger factor. They will tell you of what they fear about the countries without having been there nor even researched.

You will get a lot of suggestions that you are crazy or mad or even insane. Now most of them may be true. What then would be the definition of not living out your dreams and staying in the same place living the same day every day.

I was once driving through west Africa in a small convoy of cars. These cars were nothing special and most certainly was not 4X4's. We had with us a local guide who would see us through the rough terrain.

The area we were in was a common ground for well-known terrorists who were at that time in the market for kidnapping westerners.

During the blistering heat of the day and well into unknown territory where the sand turned to a very light and grey floury dust, which reminded me of cement before the water, we came across an old white transit van.

There were a group of unsavoury looking characters who looked like they had broken down.

As a group we decided to help them, although we took every other precaution.

For all we could see it could have been an ambush. But help we did.

The men's transit had been stranded for 5 days leaving them in a bad way with a small amount of water and little food.

The next day we met them again at a border where they treated us like hero's.

Sometimes in life you have to face the fears and dangers and with the right attitude and mind-set the rewards can be far greater than you can imagine.

Solo travel

"I am thankful for all of those who said NO to me. It's because of them I'm doing it myself."

– Albert Einstein

It can bring the most inner peace you will even gain, but it could also prove to be the loneliest time of your life.

Travelling solo either on a motorcycle or car or any other form of transport you may choose, really gets you thinking the way that you want to live. It is most definitely not for everyone but can have lasting positive effects on those who embrace it.

No deadlines or clock watching. No stepping on toes when a decision needs to be made. See, do, and go wherever and whenever you desire.

 Wherever you decide to go there will always be someone you come across that can talk some English at some level.

But there will be days and sometimes plenty of them that you will not find anyone that you can naturally converse with, and this can be quite a lonely time. It is in fact the hardest part of travelling solo. Purely because we are social creatures, and we are born and raised into social groups with social behaviours, and we have basic needs and a natural instinct to share. When there is no one there to share it with, it is going against an instinct.

I consider myself a bit of a loner and have travelled for much of my earlier years solo. Also, being a truck driver, I spent most of my time alone getting more acquainted with myself.

I learned what I really wanted in my life and have stuck to it. The long, lonely days and sometimes weeks of not talking to anyone despite trying, did get to me from time to time and deep down I knew I wanted someone to share my experiences with.

If you do travel solo, it is always best to keep a busy mind and go and do something.

WIFI is so freely available worldwide now that at your fingertips is all the knowledge you will need to give you exciting things to do and keep you busy. Every country has something to experience if you can find it.

Teams

It hit me not whilst I was travelling but whilst I was planning for another trip.

This is where I discovered overland travel for myself.

I see an advert about an adventure driving independently on a type of overland rally.

I asked a friend to join me and fell in love with this aspect of travelling that was completely new and refreshing to me. I am not saying it is a bed of roses, most certainly not. It can sometimes make you pull your hair out.

But the different opinions, aspects and assets that can vary a team are worth any challenge of annoyance.

There is more on teams in the next chapter.

The Inspiration

What are you looking for in your adventure? Are you looking to fill a gap year or put a spark in your life that you feel is missing? The so-called mid-life crisis "wink wink", and if that's so maybe I'm having one right now as I write this book. Maybe you have just become single and there's no way you want to give in to the torment of a lonesome heart.

And of course, you may be a seasoned traveller, who is looking for new paths to tread and experiences to explore that will continue to grow your lust for adventure.

Whatever your reason you must enhance your mind and soul through adventure travel, you can rest assured it is a worthy one, one that will give you the purpose and leverage you need to fulfil that burning desire to LIVE and never give in.

"The soul without imagination is what an observatory would be without a telescope."

-Henry Ward Beecher

At the beginning of every great adventure is imagination. Imagination is an architect within your soul. Henry Ward Beecher once quoted the soul without imagination is what an observatory would be without a telescope.

Now ask yourself, what excites you, what are your dreams and ambitions, what are your fears and why would you want to face them? Now make the most of your imagination, sit back, close your eyes and picture yourself fulfilling your goal. You're on the journey that you have longed for and you can hear, see, smell, taste and touch all that surrounds you, and as you listen to your emotions, notice how alive and aware you are and notice the smile on your face and the excitement all over your body.

The hardest part of adventure travel isn't whether you have the physical stamina to see your adventure through or worrying about the reputation when visiting a dangerous country. You need to ask yourself, what it is that all the great explorers have, what makes the hero rescue the maiden and in the face of fear and desperation, when all seems lost and hope has abandoned you to fend for yourself, that you don't simply lay on the floor and let the buzzards pick at your eyes. What is the force that see's the accomplishment of the goal. Well, I know for sure that a positive attitude is as important as having a parachute on a skydive. It cannot be denied that if you focus on the positives and remember your reason why you're setting out on this adventure in the first place, you will be on the right track to achieve your goal. However, a man can go a long way with a cheerful outlook, but it takes more than just seeing the bright side, you still need persistence to cross the obstacles you face and push you in the right direction towards your prize. You can never fail if you keep persisting.

The one thing you must have to see you pass over and conquer any barrier is faith. The fact that you are reading this book and imagining yourself participating in an adventure is proof enough that you have faith in yourself, that you could pull off such a task of the adventure you seek.

Are you imagining yourself climbing the highest peaks and breathing in the freshest air or white knuckling it down the Zambezi.

Whatever it is that you are thinking of at this time, it will be something that you have been longing to do. Get a pen and paper and write down what you saw, what the weather was like, what was in the background and who was there with you.

Write down what you heard, was there noise of an ocean or birds singing or was its complete silence. Did it have a distinctive smell, what did it remind you of, was it the smell of a fresh forest or meadow. How did it feel to you, was there water splashing on your face, or wind in your hair? Could you feel the long grass as you walk through lush green fields?

What was in your mind write it down now, write it rough, write fast and without thinking to long about it and then come back to this page.

When you have seen your goal and you have firmly placed it in the subconscious of your mind, you should by now have your imagination running wild.

Now is the time to set a plan. Write it down on a piece of paper and write it quick, as this is only rough thoughts from your imagination. If there is another person with you write it together and bounce of each other or do this with as many of your team as possible, the ideas you get from each will be so enlighten and it is also great fun.

"Metaphors have a way of holding the most truth in the least space."

- Orson Scott Card

Life is a Happy, Exciting Adventure. Using metaphors can have a profound effect on your life and outlook. Find a metaphor that suits how you want to be and where you want to be in the future. What is life to you? Make it positive and empowering.

You can use metaphors towards any part of life and particularly in your travel adventures. If you think of adventure travel as a fear for the unknown or a tough slog to get to a destination, that is exactly what you will get. But think of it as an incredible learning experience of excitement, whilst getting to your destination and it would greatly enhance the quality of your entire journey.

Not putting it off any longer and doing what you desire most, will give you a profound sense of overwhelming achievement, an inner self pride and even a humbleness for life. But most of all a "right what's next" attitude towards travel.

Chapter 3

Planning my 5-Ps Planning and Preparation prevents poor performance

"I run on the road, long before I dance under the lights." -Muhammad Ali

When all the ideas are in and written down, read them back to yourself a few times and then start planning to detail. I say detail what I really mean is everything but your route. If you want a planned detailed route, you can find many organised guided tour companies that will have this already done and you can throw away your pen and get your wallet out.

But if you are looking to see the real world your way, on your terms and your experiences then your desire to find what you want to see and experience within your journey will map out the route for you. It will never be as the crow flies. Meaning that if time is permitting see and do all you can but prioritise the must see's and do's and leaving time for the I wonder what's over there's.

"Research is what I'm doing when I don't know what I'm doing."

-Wernher von Braun

In July 2014 whilst driving through Turkey in a team of five people, one of the team as he was looking through a guidebook, came across a world heritage site called Mount Nimrod. It took two full days out of our schedule and also it took its toll on our vehicle, because of the narrow, steep and rough, rocky road that led us to the 2140m summit. The heat of southern Turkey was extreme as all, but a driver had to walk the last couple of km's, so that our van with a lightened load and a bit of extra horsepower had more of a chance of climbing the sloping gravelled tracks. Eventually upon reaching the top we were in awe of the ancient monument that stood before us as though it was waiting to be wondered over.

Having seen this for myself I felt the need to research a little and the most reliable and accurate source I found on the subject was with the World monuments fund. Not to dwell on this too much, if you feel the need, please look up this fascinating story.

What I will say is that this adventure turned out to be a key point and a worthy use of our time and effort and if we stuck to a well organised planned route, this experience would have passed us by.

Creating a well-balanced team

"It is amazing how much you can accomplish

when it doesn't matter who gets the credit".

-Harry S Truman

It is human nature to travel in groups. Since man has travelled vast distances and explored new lands, he as felt the need to share his findings and experiences.

From the age of Twenty-one until I was Thirty seven, I spent most of my time visiting destinations that I had a burning desire to see, alone. Going where I want, when I want, I met so many friends and gained experiences that would have lasting effects on my life, even the bad ones which of course were all part of the teachings that adventure travel brings.

I knew that returning home to London was also a highlight as I would get to tell close ones of my adventures. But the sharing never lasted, and a sigh was dispersed from the lips of the person that I thought I was amusing with my yarns.

Everyone wants to tell their story but if you have done what they haven't it's a Herculean task to get any interest out of them.

Having others to share your experiences also gives you confidence to gain and do more experiences. You laugh more and with the combined know how of all your team you see more of the things you could have missed out on. You also learn more as you will spend time discussing and fact finding on the subject you have just met.

You will all have different views on a matter and knowledge from different experiences that will add different and enlighten aspects towards it.

It will be tempting to invite a friend or family member to join you on quest, but You will need to use your judgement. I have personal experience in using bad judgement and invited into the team a character, who after long periods in the company of the team, combined with hot temperatures and potentially stressful situations, took it upon themselves to judge and condemn fellow teammates, without judging themselves first. It caused stress, anger, and a lot of resentment. Not what you should be looking for in your team of leaders.

There are many websites, forums, and social pages you can find or advertise for team members.

- Have they a positive and pleasing personality?

- What are their strong points and assets that would be of benefit to the team?

- Do they have the time needed for the journey and of course can they afford it?

If a worthy friend says they would love to participate but the timing is wrong, sometimes it is worth the wait.

Having a plan B if a team member needs to pull out and believe me it happens a lot, again bide your time and seek out an adventurer who is most suited for your journey.

Being part of a team can be a great challenge of minds in itself. Having experienced this myself, I found that many weeks confided to a small space in hostile environments such as corrupt border crossings to navigation errors can test patience's of the calmest of saints.

Do not condemn, moan, criticise or blame, but instead find room for encouragement and praise. We all love to hear it and it picks us up and pushes us forward.

Lead by example and inspire others to do and be what it takes to work. This is not going to be easy but with patience and belief in your team could be extremely rewarding.

When you start drawing up detailed plans of your adventure, remember to always keep in mind your goal. Always recheck that your plans are complimentary to your desired purpose.

Research your interest thoroughly, discover what you could learn that will intensify what you are trying to find in yourself.

Make it a team effort

Teamwork divides the task and doubles the success.

Involving the team into the creation of a route, will give you various aspects and thoughts. Taking the best and most popular attractions from the whole group will give the whole team more inspiration and involvement. It can also be another excuse to gather the team together and gel with one another.

Never do an expedition or any lengthy journey with a team member who is happy to be just going along for the ride. As eventually everyone will want to make some sort of contribution, it is one of our basic human needs, the need of significance or feeling important. All your team members should be able to serve a purpose otherwise over time they will feel left out and resentful, they may even be resented by other team members and friction between the team will become tense and stressful.

Choosing your team should be made a priority decision at the beginning of your preparation.

Plan for the law of the land

Some countries have laws, traditions, and a lot of frowning upon. Be sure to check and list anything you feel maybe an issue for you. But as long as your always sincerely polite and courteous with a cheerful smile, you won't go far wrong.

Planning any overland expedition or adventurous journey can be daunting and you could start getting overwhelmed. You will become irritable and probably curse way too much. You will need to remind yourself that the actual adventure will be and should be many times tougher. To tackle these situations of annoyance, I would suggest writing all that you need to do into a list and then prioritise the most urgent and important first, i.e.:

- Your team

- Your vehicle

- Sponsorship, if of course you need any support for your achievement.

If you're planning your journey at short notice, then passports and any visas that you may need would full into the priority category.

When you have prioritised your list, break it down into smaller parts, that are more manageable and easier to complete. You should start planning well in advance of your adventure to cover for any obstacles and there will be many.

Time

Time as a wonderful way of showing us what really matters

-Margaret Peters

Time is an important factor and whether it is time preparing or time indulging in your adventure, time is of the essence. Leaving plenty of space and room for error for your team in the preparation of the journey and a steadfast attitude towards your list, will result in a less stressed, less overwhelmed group and give you the luxury of adding other items of benefit to your expedition.

There is no time like the present

During your fulfilment of your list, you will come across obstacles, there is no denying it, it will happen. You should use it as practice to keep a calm mind as frustration will only blur your thoughts and create a bigger obstruction for yourself.

It is not worth moaning about it or making excuses not to do it. The best way to solve a problem is simply to solve the problem.

If possible, ask the rest of your team for their thoughts on the matter. If you are travelling on your own, then have no hesitation and blinker yourself to the problem at hand until it is resolved, or you have answers.

Calmly and persistently handle whatever situation that is in front of you as soon as possible. Then continue with your list as this will keep you focused on your goal.

With any extreme adventure or expedition that crosses borders and continents, there is an exceedingly high possibility that things might not go the way of the hopeful. Be prepared to be up front with your boss, be sincere and explain your likely hood of an extended break. If for instance your maximum vacation time is 2 months, then plan the adventure for five or possibly six weeks to completion. As you should allow yourself a minimum of two days before departing. This will get you off on the right foot so as not to be rushing and keeping a calm head.

Having a full-time job where you are employed by a company especially large corporation's or one with strict rules on holidays and time off has its downfalls when it comes to the actual length of your adventure. I have come across this on many occasions when one or more team members has a deadline to meet and tries to fit the expedition within that deadline.

On every occasion that I have witnessed it has had the same results, stress, and tension within the group. Not just on the one who is in a rush to get back to their desk of insanity but is prepared to cause the rest of the team to miss out as it will influence scenic routes or short cuts or stopping to have a look around and seeing what is down that track.

You should also allow yourselves a minimum of one week during your travels. In the likely hood of breakdowns, extended border crossing and my favourite staying in a magnificent location a day or so longer, where this would be a great way to relieve any tensions and help solve any vehicle or navigation issues.

Upon arriving home from a life changing experience, you should give yourself at least a week to settle down, as your emotions will be running on full power you will need to tell everyone everything, but it will seem that no one understands unless they have experienced similar. The best way is to be humble about your experience and use it to provide logic to a situation, it would prove much more appreciative to others who have never done what you have just done.

63

Going straight back to the grindstone of your place of employment is a waste of time as your mind would almost defiantly will not be on the job. As it is time you should be reflecting and coming back down to earth with a smile on your face instead of having to face the arduous task of putting your adventure out of your head and getting down to work.

The bad news is time flies. The good news is you're the pilot.

-Michael Altshuler.

Budget and keeping track of it

"Life is a game and money is how we keep score"

- Ted Turner

A fool and his money are easily parted and running out of funds halfway through your journey is quite literally one of the most irresponsible things you could do. Check your budget on a daily basis as it will become a negative burden between you and your teammates who will feel obliged to help you out.

If they say it's OK, I don't mind, you can rest assured that feeling will go after a week or even a few days.

You will end up being left out of excursion and well needed nights on the town. So, if you are a person who loves to spend freely with no account for your budget, may I suggest you take a good DVD player for all your lonely nights in.

A simple planner that is easy to follow and view in times when there is not 't much to do, is a good option.

Example

Days	Daily budget	Daily spending	Spare + /Overspent -
1	£/$67	80	13-
2	67	40	27+
3	67	16	51+
4	67	121	54-
5	67	56	11+
6	67	68	1+
7	67	56	11

	week 1	437	469
			Total = 32+
(Saving the $32 for times of need could prove to save the day)			
68	1-		

8	67		
9	67	50	17+
10	67	79	12-
11	67	84	17-
12	67	80	13-
13	67	68	1-
14	67	63	4+
		week 2	492 469
			Total = 23-

(It's good practice not to dip into to the spare money, instead take it from the previous weeks budget)

15	63	80	17-
16	63	48	15+
17	63	50	13+
18	63	76	13-

124	67	100	33-
125	67	56	11-

Within your planning you will have written down an itinerary of your journey and what you would like to see and do.

It would be worth writing down under it what is necessary and what would be a bonus if you have the resources.

Budget for the must do's and do your best to save on your budget so the bonus becomes a treat.

Looking for bargains and cheaper options whilst shopping and never be afraid to haggle with local retailers (you may surprize yourself) could save so much money and could even give you some much needed equipment.

Even looking for the cheaper fuel stations could prove to be a budget booster. Make a note on the price on fuel as you go and work out the average and always try to beat the lowest.

In each of the subjects within the planning, there are ways on saving money that could help you to experience more on your expedition.

Keep your money safe!

I like to have the assurance of a credit card in case my cash supplies are lost. It has not happened as yet, but I have turned this into a sort of ritual. It will get you out of a potentially tricky situation, in a worst-case scenario.

If you are going into a situation that as a risk of robbery, it is best to spread your money around instead of keeping it together.

There are many new hidden compartments in clothing, belts, shoes and so on now a days that would make it make easier to conceal your goods.

Waist belts or pouches can be a dead giveaway and even an encouragement for a would be crook. As you rummage into it to find some change to pay for lunch, always be aware of who is standing around you.

Crooks will always produce new and inventive ways to steal from you.

It would not be worth me writing down what to look for in a potential robbery because there are so many ways a thief will steal from you, but prevention is better than the cure.

Be aware of what looks like an unpleasant situation. Crossroads or walk into more crowded places. If possible, walk in groups or at least in twos.

Try never to stand out as a target. i.e.: Unfolding your giant map down a back street in Buenos Aires or looking through and taking money from your waist belt in the middle of the road is asking for trouble.

I would say to you avoid more run-down areas, but sometimes these places hold the real culture of a place. So, go there with an open mind and a confidence stance. Remember to make friends and a have a pleasing personality and take enjoyment and experience from your surroundings.

Routes

Your route and what you want to achieve on the way

From the outset you will probably know where you want to go and where to leave from. You have in your imagination worked out the reason you want to achieve this.

Drawing up a route is without any doubt the most imaginative part of any expedition or adventure. As you quite literally see yourself there on your travels.

There are tools available to you now that would have made Sir Walter Raleigh weep into his ruff.

Google earth and Google maps to name just two, will virtually walk you through your route and picture all you want to see and do.

Keep your route realistic and within your time limits. Remembering the unexpected will always crop up. You will get lost no matter how good your navigation skills and tools are. You will also experience breakdowns, punctures, leaks and whatever can go wrong will go wrong. Plans will change, and it never rains until pours, how is that for negative thinking for you. And if you expect it to happen, more than likely it will happen. But if you take the negative and turn it into a positive by being open minded and welcome them as opportunities to improve you will undoubtedly get better and better. So, the next time you face an obstacle that others see as a setback you will be prepared and on top of any situation and the more experienced and knowledgeable you will become.

All is lost

"The best way to solve a problem is simply to solve the problem."

-The Author

The best thing about when all is lost, and it's all gone belly up is that they are the times that will be remembered the most. As it is a natural instinct for people to talk about them and to add the hardship as a great adventure and experience that most of the time they laugh about, (in the future).

I have taken tours on overland adventures in the past when on that day nothing seemed to go right.

There were breakdowns, burst pipes 22 hours of driving and a freezing cold mountain night approaching. Yes, it was not in the brochure, but we all survived, tired but un-scaved and to our destination.

For the rest of the weeks travelling, it was one of the biggest single topics of conversation and everyone felt they had achieved something. Really people love to talk about hardship experiences it gives them a sense of importance and in fact most make it into a competition.

Always focus on your goal

It is such a key factor that you keep in mind the reason you're participating in your journey in the first place, and you will see it written about in this book on more than one occasion.

Make your goal come to life, whether it is to see places you have longed to see or discover your true calling in life. It maybe that you are looking to become more spiritual, and you are seeking something more.

Whatever your desire to travel is make it big and bright and bring it to your mind as often as possible, in particular in times of stress and frustration.

73

Keep an open mind.

Planning a route needs to bring out the creative magician in you, as to keep everyone happy you will have to create magic. You are probably better off with a dart and a blind fold and hope for the best.

You need a start and a finish point, which you should do your best to stick to, but even these can change. As earlier in this chapter when I spoke about our trek up Mt Nemrod you need to be loose with your route. Keep on course to the next finish or check point which could be a border crossing or town but allow time for diversions. Moreover, if it takes five days to reach the border, then give yourself seven. You will need to keep this in mind when you are applying for visas, because you will not want to outstay your welcome.

Take time out to smell the roses

The reason most of us travel is not just so we can brag about it to less fortunate friends who don't have the passion of adventure as you do. Or to give you the sense that you think your friends are filled with respect for you and that now you are a well-travelled Yoda, of course not. Because if anything they are bored with your yarns and feeling slightly jealous. So, it is better to be humble and speak of your travels when they can add value to a conversation or situation.

Leading to the main reason a let us say, "seasoned traveller" travels, is freedom.

It is sitting on a cliff edge looking across a stunning valley or floating down a river in a canoe that was crafted by native Amazonian Indians.

It could be travelling over oceans to see a Blue whale and feeling a sense of self achievement and yes even an enlightenment and it's yours that no one can take from you and you haven't even got to share it because you will always keep the feeling you had at that moment in time.

So, when planning your route take care to add plenty of opportunities to take time out and breathe the air, feel alive and embrace the freedom.

If you do not take anything else from this book, take this paragraph as it is the source of all wisdom in adventure travel.

Maps

Sat-navs and map apps are good and fairly reliable, until they are not. Big cities with a mass of skyscrapers, forest and mountain ranges are no friend to our satellite navigation systems.

However, in this modern high-tech world of ours, there are plenty of offline apps, such as google offline maps, which proved to be very dependable and just takes some WIFI to download an area and off you go.

There is also maps.me which I have had to use whilst working for an overland tour company through south America. They are good in a lot of respects but no separate directions for a 26 ton, 14-foot-high, 35' long truck and it seemed to be in love with low bridges and narrow streets with a dead end. It also lost signal a fair amount of the time. In a car or van, I would say it is OK but don't rely on it too much and do a lot more alternative route planning.

So, take the good old paper maps for the whole of your travels. Take a superior quality compass and at least one spare.

If no one has any orientation skills. There are plenty of quick guides to map and compass survival. It is always best to know something and improve than nothing at all.

You can save money by looking around for the cheapest maps. Amazon or eBay is a good place to start.

I myself usually go to these platforms to buy my maps and spend around two or three dollars per map.

Travel guides can be found on these sites at much cheaper prices than any high Street.

Check the news

On a journey to Timbuktu all was well. Everything was prepared, and we headed off for the town that became a myth and a metaphor for far and distant lands (from here to Timbuktu).

Whilst traveling through Western Sahara with limited internet connections, we heard of the abduction of four tourist, one of which was shot dead for refusing to get into the kidnapper's vehicle. This was one incident among many that had been happing in the area over the previous months. We were then advised, and advice I took because the want for still wanted to have more life to live and more travelling to do out weighted anything else, to steer clear of that whole area. We then changed our plans and routes and headed towards Gambia Instead.

It turned out to be a blessing and an amazing experience, one which I would well recommend.

Checking government and related websites for updates on dangerous areas and no-go areas and also including whether, should be made part and parcel of an adventure travellers' skills, one that which could save the day.

In many high-altitude countries, the weather changes within minutes, so any source of information on this will not always be totally dependable.

Guide books

When I travel through a country I have never been to before. I like nothing better than to read up about it. It gets you to understand more about the culture and history. The story of an ancient city or mystery of a deserted ghost town always intrigues me.

They are also useful to find the best places to eat, sleep and find local attractions and watering holes.

you can also find some extremely useful information on the local laws and traditions.

If at all possible, it is always best to get the latest copy of a guidebook.

Wherever you go in the world, changes are a plenty. Road closures, buildings shut down and the politics of the country sometimes can change everything.

I do always try to get a colour copy of a guide, because they add a bit more vibrancy and reality to what you're hoping to see and learn.

Your Vehicle

Travelling across continents on an overland adventure can be a life changing experience. It could test all of your resources to the limits and on completion to your destiny feel you with pride, confidence, a great sense of achievement and of course knowledge.

Above all the significant choice of the vehicle must be an appropriate one if you are going to have this chance of success.

It is however not always best to have the best vehicle. Through driving vehicles across undrivable terrain and breaking them to submission is a worthy challenge for even the most dedicated overlander.

When you fix it time and time again and then finish by driving it to its destination against all the odds and ridicules, it is time to punch the air and feel worthy at being a true overland adventurer.

Choosing your vehicle

When looking for the perfect vehicle for your challenge first of all you want to look at what you want to achieve and your route.

If of course you want to be driving through Europe or North America in the summer, then a normal family saloon would be plenty good enough.

The trunks are usually big enough for all your luggage or you could even pull a small trailer behind you.

This would make it much easier for you to get around and see what you want to see with much less bother.

Going in the winter would be a different story. In some places you would not only need a 4x4 you would also have to use snow chains and extra equipment for surviving the conditions.

Driving through Asia, Africa, or South America it would probably be best advised to use a 4x4 as the roads can in some places be car killers.

When looking to buy a vehicle try never to rush into it and get the first one you see.

It is always best to give yourself plenty of time to search for the ideal vehicle for your needs.

On the times I have driven through Africa I have researched the route and decided that a small, short wheelbase 4x4 would be quite sufficient enough for two people with all their kit, tools and equipment.

Upon driving through central Asia this time there was five in my team, so I had to think differently.

I checked the route, the distance, the length of time we had and considered the conditions of the roads.

The first part of the journey was through Europe and of course the roads in Europe are easy with very few difficulties.

Once you start getting into Asia there are still roads that are tarmac and in good condition or most parts driveable for at least two thirds of the total distance.

These roads usually run out and get replaced by the tracks. Mongolia was particularly bad or good (depending on the adventure you are looking) for this and throughout the roads were not even tracks but dried out rivers and sort of paths that were made by vehicles driving aimlessly nowhere.

The majority of the time you will have to carve out your own pathway with your vehicle.

My team and I decided on a van. I travelled locally and some distance until I was happy with what we needed.

Even though the van I bought had bad reviews I went to look and discover for myself. As I approached the driveway next to the seller's house, was an LDV Maxus. It looked in extremely good condition and was an ex-postal vehicle. After checking it over and giving it a broad inspection I knew that I had a bargain.

The Maxus got a conversion and a complete overhaul. Now it was very suitable for all of us.

It's also became my favourite vehicle I have ever taken overland it seemed to go over everything and despite the roughness and what that poor van had to go through, the only mishap was a broken suspension arm, which was due to some very poor driving.

Maintaining

keeping your vehicle in working order is an essential part of your journey.

Doing a 15 to 20 min check could make the difference to your challenge.

Below is a check list you should use to keep your vehicle in good shape.

Regular vehicle check list

1) **Brakes**. You should take with you a spare set off brake pads or shoes and check at least once a week or more frequently depending on the roughness of the terrain including dust and dirt that could get behind the brake shoes.

2) **Brake pipes**. Pipes can always break and fracture, again when travelling over rough ground stones can flick up and fracture pipes.

3) **Tyres.** Rough terrain can damage and puncture tyres. They can also shred and tear. Sand can quickly wear down tyres as it acts like sandpaper.

4) **Wheel nuts.** When a vehicle is bouncing around on rough roads it can loosen nuts and bolts. If you have recently changed a wheel, you should then tighten the nuts after a least two hours of driving and also after driving on rough roads.

5) **Suspension.** suspension legs can also loosen when they are rigorously Shaken and therefore can wear the bolt and even come loose. This would include bushes that can brake and crack. You should carry a whole bunch of them.

6) **Greasing.** There are usually grease nipples on the steering column, the prop, and the wheels. You should take a grease gun with plenty of grease with you and re-grease when needed but before they go dry.

7) **Exhaust.** Check from time to time the condition of the exhaust. You could hear it if it were rattling and see it and smell it, if it had a leak. you can buy some exhaust tape that could get you out of trouble. With a broken exhaust you can lose some important power from the engine, which can also cost more in fuel.

8) **Lights.** Make sure you have enough spare bulbs with you and that you check your lights are working all around your vehicle on a regular basis.

9) **Windscreen and mirrors.** It would be far too expensive and space consuming to take a spare windscreen and mirrors with you. But there are ways that you could repair in an emergency. For the wing mirrors good old duct tape or cable ties work wonders. For the windscreen sandpaper and a good resin or even super glue can usually stop a crack becoming worse.

10) **Oil.** You should check your oil levels regularly, as to much usage could be telling you there is a problem with the engine. Also, for leaks and to see if there is any water entering the oil system. Always get the appropriate oil for your vehicle and try not to cheapskate.

11) **Water.** You should check your water levels and for water leaks every day. There are some good techniques and applications you can use to stop leaks. It's also good practice to use an antifreeze to help lubricate and maintain a longer life to the water pipeline.

12) **Battery.** Check that the battery is tight and in place and the connections are not loose. Make sure the battery is being charged and not going flat. If this is the case it may be the Alternator that is the problem so first check any loose connections. The battery may also require a top up of distilled water.

13) **Fuel leaks.** When the bonnet is open have a look, and smell around for signs of a fuel leak. These can usually be cured with tape or re-cutting of a pipe.

14) **Fluids.** Other fluids in the vehicle such as transmission can cause a problem. So, check for levels and leaks.

15) **Air filter.** After driving through thick dust and sand your air filter could get clogged and not be efficient. This can affect the air intake of the engine and not have enough to burn causing the vehicle to stall. sometimes putting an extra layer over the intake such as a sock or other clothing can help this.

16) **Gears.** Making sure your gears work as they should, and the clutch and brake fluid are topped up, which is an especially important part of maintenance. So, regularly check levels. Driving technique is often a

cause for gears playing up. Do not ride the clutch and practise smooth changing with the clutch fully depressed.

17) **Handbrake.** If you have a faulty handbrake without you knowing could leave you in a bit of a mess, especially on hills. So, check it at least once a week.

Tools

It is always best to carry enough tools for the job. When I say tools, I do not just mean a set of spanners, I mean the right tools and equipment that will get you out of trouble.

It's no good taking a garage load of tools that will overload your vehicles weight limit, but to take what could be essential.

Below is a guided list of items that could be essential kit for your vehicle.

- **Cable ties.** Can be used to hold many things together. They can also keep together luggage and other equipment or used for tightening around pipes.

- **Duct tape, Gaffer, and Insulation tape.** Essential for burst pipes, electrical faults, ripped roofs or a thousand other essentials that may come up.

- **Liquid metal.** I found this to be extremely useful on exhaust systems, radiators, and anything metal with a whole in it where no whole should have been.

- **Tow rope and additional rope.** For obvious reasons take a tow rope. There will very often be a friendly local who could get you out of stook and good karma if you can help someone else who has got themselves stranded.

- **Bottle jack and two pieces of strong solid wood.** A bottle jack takes up less room and lifts more weight than a trolley jack. You will need the wood as a base to put the jack on to stop it sinking in soft mud or sand.

- **Snow chains.** Getting an excellent quality set of snow chains is highly recommended and can be very useful and noticeable in extreme weather conditions. If all else fails and there are not any chains in your kit, you could try using rope. Tie it around and through your tyres and wheels evenly space and as tight as you can.

- **Shovels.** A good pair of shovels are particularly useful when stuck in mud, snow, or sand. Good for digging a quick latrine or fire pit also.

- **Carpet.** If weight is an issue, then **sand ladders** can be a hindrance, as they are certainly not light. An alternative is a rug or piece of old carpet. I actually prefer this as it's lighter and easier to carry. If you get stuck, remember to use the rope to tie to the rug and the rear of the car, so when you have driven over the rug it will follow you out and prevent you having to stop to retrieve it.

- **Grease and grease gun.** To lubricate parts that are drying out or deteriorate. Good for waterproofing when in high levels of water. Wheel nuts and other nuts and bolts, to make easier removal when needed. Battery terminals should also be greased.

- **Gasket sealant.** You can find gasket sets that are universal and can be cut to shape. Although I would recommend that you do bring the right head gasket with you. Doing this stopped a teammate and myself having to abandon our vehicle, somewhere in the Sahara.

- **Socket set, Spanners, Screw drivers, Club hammer.** I like to go shopping at a local car boot sale for quality but dirt-cheap tools. It's good for a haggle too.

- **Puncture repair.** These are things you can get from a tyre sponsor, Such as ATS who gave me Twenty sets of repair kits for free.

- **Spare bulbs.** Some of the roads you may pass could be deadly and scary enough during the day, let alone driving them in the dark. Practise changing them before you leave as you may never know when they might go.

- **Spare belts.** Unless you have an endless supply of tights/pantyhose, then take some spare belts with you. If you have had the vehicle serviced fully before you left, then the cam belt should have been changed and that should be sound unless of course you are driving heavily for over 6 months then take a spare. Alternator and fan belts are a must and if possible, the power steering belt.

- **Super glue.** Great alternative to fix small punctures, broken luggage, and even temporary repair to the windscreen.

- **A file.** Handy in making tight bolts easier to screw in.

- **A funnel.** You will want to take a couple of funnels with you. Topping up fluids of different sorts is much more efficient.

- **Jerry Cans.** Here would be a good idea to calculate the longest distance you will be travelling, where there are no signs of civilisation. It is rare nowadays to be completely isolated from others, but when travelling across vast deserts, mountain ranges or salt plains it is better to be safe than sorry. You will need to take a sufficient amount of fuel with you. A 20ltr jerry can would get you around 160-200 miles, depending on fuel type, (more if diesel) and driving habits. So, if you are planning to go overland for more than the vehicles fuel tank range, where there is no place to refuel. Then take enough jerry cans to fill up with you.

- **Bungee straps.** I do love a bungee strap; they are always handy for holding many things in place or even washing lines. I also put one around my backpack so that I can identify it at airport lost luggage claims.

- **Core plugs.** These can go without warning. They are not expensive, and you can get an assortment of them. If one goes then your engine will overheat in no time. Also, it could help other overland travellers who have been caught out.

- **Fire extinguisher.** I think you could imagine what could happen if you don't have one. If you catch a fire early enough, you could prevent a small battery fire turning into a raging inferno and a very spoiled adventure.

- **Vaseline.** Use this as a sealant to put around electrical components if you are having to cross rivers or water ways.

- **Wheel brace.** If you forget your wheel brace, prepare for a lengthy walk.

- **Crowbar.** You never know when you need the leverage of a crowbar. It could save the day.

- **Fluids.** This should be part of your daily checks whilst travelling. Take decent quality fluids, which have better density to them, so they do a more efficient job.

- **Sand paper.** It's good for cleaning plugs and points and as many other usages.

- **Hose pipe.** Siphoning fuel from your jerry cans is a lot less effort than lifting it while you fill up for five minutes. Also in many developing countries, it is common to fill up from a barrel and you should expect to be using this method more than you think.

Whatever your vehicle, it is an essential part of your planning. Whether your mode of transport is a car, bus, train, paramotor glider, horse or even your own legs, you will need to make the necessary arrangements of documents, insurance, maintenance knowledge and whatever that vehicle needs for a successful adventure.

Vehicle Documents

When you are participating on an adventure in a vehicle you need to make sure your paperwork is up to scratch. For your own safety, be sure it has a road safety certificate and registration documents.

Some countries require an international driving permit a lot do not.

Also, in countries such as Iran you will need to purchase a Carnet de passage. Which is similar to having a passport for your vehicle and a promise that you will take your vehicle with you upon leaving the country.

Carnets are extremely expensive but if you are planning to explore a whole country which requires one, it is certainly better to have one and have more freedom to sight see the harder to reach places than to not have one.

The other alternative is to arrange a fixer. Usually, a local guide or agent that will arrange safe passage for you, but it will restrict your route and they usually set out a route for you to follow. Boring but cheaper if your budget is tight and you just want to transit through.

A green card is needed in places such as Turkey and gives your vehicle insurance and freedom to travel.

When arranging your vehicle insurance, you will need to complete it before you leave and take it on the road. This is necessary when passing though developed countries. When travelling through lesser developed countries insurances can be purchased at border crossings in the form of a ticket or green card. Be prepared to negotiate a lower price because you can be assured, they will try to negotiate a higher price.

I have travelled for weeks before without insurance in some parts of Africa, not because of a budget or avoidance, but because it seemed a laborious task for certain border guards, unless he had his bite of the cherry. So, stick to your guns, I was never asked again.

I would highly recommend, particularly if driving though Africa that you print out at least 30 - 50 Fiche forms for every week of your stay. Fiche are forms with all your information on (see sample on next page) and are vital as you will be stopped at endless check points throughout your journey.

If you do not have fiche forms, you will have to hand over all your documents to be checked. Which would cause much wear and tear on your documents, and excuse to ask for a bribe. Handing over a fiche will save much unnecessary frustration.

Below is an example fiche form that you can copy and enter your details on

Nom: *Name:* *Add Photo HERE!*	
Domicile: *Address:*	*321 Any road* *Any town* *Any county, any postal code*
Date *Date* **de** **naissance:***of Birth*	*01/01/1968*
Lieu *place* **de** **naissance:** *of Birth*	*London*
Nationalité: *Nationality:*	*English*
Numéro *passport* **de** *Number:***passeport:**	

Date/*Date* **d'émmission:** *of Issue:*	*20/05/2003*
Date/*Date* **d'échéance:** *of Expiry:*	*20/05/2013*
profession: Occupation:	*Truck Driver*
Nom-Mother de Name: Mère:	*Mothers name*
Nom-Fathers de Name: PÈRE:	*Fathers Name*
Marque/Make de of la Car: voiture:	*Suzuki SJ410*
NuméroRegistration *d'enregistrement: No.:*	*F123OLD*
Date Registrationd'enregistrement: *Vin Date:*	*26/08/88* *VSEOSJJ2D0119876* *5*
Date d'entrée of Entry intodans *Country: le pays: Date*	*Date of entry into* *country*
Lieu d'entrée of Entry dans into *Country le pays:* *place*	*Place*

Know your vehicle!

Within your team should be a wide range of knowledge that would be an asset to your expedition.

One of these assets should be knowledge of the vehicle and I mean more than just being able to change a tyre.

It is well worth you or another team member to take a few basic vehicle maintenance lessons. Also available is YouTube where you can simply type in the make and model of your vehicle, and someone somewhere would have made a video on how to maintain it.

It is fun to learn as you go, and boy, do you learn fast. But if you find yourself in the middle of a desert bogged down, axle deep in sand and help is days away or worst non-existent. Then knowing a little thing such as deflating your types to spread the traction may be the difference between life or death.

Try not to neglect the importance of vehicle maintenance it could quite literally save your life.

Accommodation

Depending on what you have planned your accommodation could be anything from a five-star luxury hotel to a hammock under the stars.

It depends also on your funds and budget and location, meaning that sometimes you have no choice but to get a room because there may be no place to camp.

If you have an RV or motor home, then looking for a place to park such as a shopping mall car park could be easier to find than a camp site.

Sticking to your budget can mean shopping around a bit. If of course it's a busy weekend or there is a large event happening, you can usually find somewhere cheaper.

If there is plenty of available accommodation never be afraid to haggle and get the best deal for you and your budget.

Seeing that travelling in a motor home or staying in hotels does not require you to be Rambo, I have made some simple suggestions about some basic camping skills that could be of use.

Basic camping skills

There are many stories of people you have survived situations of being stranded or lost in the wilderness. Most of the time it comes from sheer desire to live. But if that is lost then so are your chances. If you have a bit of know-how and some survival skills it gives you an edge and a boost that can push you through any negative position, I am saying it is better to know something than nothing at all.

Depending on the scale and difficulty of your overland adventure you should gain some basic skills that could help make you and your team's life that bit easier and more productive and hopefully enjoyable.

Camp etiquette is more important than you may think, especially on long arduous journeys where any small annoying habits can spark an argument (the straw that broke the camel's back).

You don't have to go to the expense of attending a course you could simply buy a good book.

You should never compromise with cheap undervalued equipment, which includes books.

Get one with good and honest reviews that as a lot to offer. To save money you could buy it second hand. I would recommend a book called the complete illustrated handbook of survival. It is well written with clear example pictures. It's not the smallest book in the world but it's worth exchanging a couple of spare shirts in your ruck sack for.

Take from it some basic skills such as setting up a camp, lighting a fire, camp cooking, cleanliness in the camp and probably the most important, making a brew. Simple you may think but it's all down to the timing.

If the worst does happen via a sickness, accident or even any hostile situation, I will say it again, it is better to know something than nothing at all.

What most of these books do not say is, it is about your own mental state. Breathe, keep a calm head, and ask yourself questions, on the best way you can overcome your situation. Ask enough questions and you will find an answer.

I have been at borders where you are surrounded by people who have nothing and want you to help them, although more often than not want to help you in exchange of something. Which is fine if you have something they ca help with. This can be very intimidating when you are surrounded. Then there are the ones without a conscious. At the first opportunity the extremely corrupt officials, will openly and proudly take everything that you have.

These can be incredibly stressful times and letting it get to you with an angry mind state will almost certainly make the situation worst.

Where a calm, focused and positive outlook and mind will certainly improve the situation. It is all part of overland travel.

I would always recommend someone or if possible two or more team members have some **first aid skills**. It could happen when you are least expecting it. If you are not prepared and in the middle of absolute nowhere, death is always a possibility, where knowing some first aid could have helped. It maybe you that needs the help.

Where to camp

Finding the right spot for your camp takes a bit of practise. It is not just a matter of here looks good and throw your tent up. Using your skills and wisdom you will be able to determine that it is better to set up camp before dark. If you see a suitable place along the way grab it there and then. Even if your limited for time as it would be more beneficial to the team and the goal if you had a good night's rest and leave earlier than it would to keep driving until it's a must to stop. It is then a rush to eat, there is more stress, it's dark and you usually have no idea what your surroundings are like and worst of all you don't have time to relax with your team and take in the moment.

It is always good practise to keep an eye on the weather looking at the sky for tell-tale clouds.

There is a lot to tell on whether and its unpredictability. But be prepare and where ever possible check local weather forecast. This can also help you decide where to set up your camp.

There are many countries with campsite areas, but I find them to be less of an attraction as they are usually in an out of the way corner, they have absolutely no view and with so much rubbish it would give the Wombles a bad day.

Firstly, if you are travelling through a hostile country, make sure you are not setting up camp in a mind field, as you do not want to be visiting the little boy's room in the middle of the night and wake up the whole neighbourhood.

What you do want to look for is relatively flat high ground that is well drained. If in a hot country some shade would help keep the camp cooler. If a cold country, look for some shelter from the wind. Camping high will also help avoid pockets of cold air.

If camping near water, make sure to be above the tidal or flood line.

Camping in forest as it is dangers also and can easily flood and have a risk of falling branches that are broken or rotten.

Keeping your camp tidy and putting away food is an essential part of good camping etiquette. It will attract bugs or much larger creatures. If you don't have airtight containers and even if you do, it is best to store leftovers and other open foods high and out the way of the camp.

If you do happen to come across something that sees you as breakfast, you must remain calm as panic will not help.

It should be made common practice to have a doing's bag in the tent with you. I call it a doing's bag because it will have all the necessary things you will need when getting into your tent at night.

Such things as a torch and head torch, bottled water, and something to read or write on and with. If on cold nights, you may want an extra pair of socks or shirt. You may also want a pack of cards with you if you are sharing your tent.

Food and Equipment

Food and water are essential to success.

Food is an essential part of the planning, whatever size of your expedition or adventure. It will increase in importance the more rigorous it may be. Such as long treks across extreme and challenging terrains.

Having a good solid nutritional meal at the start and end of the day, will keep your strength and energy levels high.

It helps with keeping the spirits and morale up, even in the harshest of conditions.

Buy essential food wherever possible on your journey. Such as local markets and stores.

You will need to calculate the amount needed for the whole team in between stop overs. Buy extra if possible and stick to the diet set out, do not gorge in moments of weakness as this could be the difference of overspending on your budget and having food when you need it most.

Remember to store plenty of fats, proteins, vitamins, and minerals and even cellulose. Although it does not get broken down in our bodies, it helps us digest food. Essential on long haul expeditions to avoid constipation.

Dried food is lightweight, simple to pack and relatively easy to cook. Rice and pasta are good sources of carbohydrates and can be very tasty when mixed with sauces and fresh vegetables. They are also cheap for a energy boost. However, carbohydrates should not be the main source of food has they are a temporary fix for hunger. Fats and dairy will sustain energy levels over longer periods. Chocolate can be used as a welcomed treat and will be psychological boost in times of hardship.

Some things to remember when preparing your food for your journey.

- **The size of your team:** This will regulate the number of rations needed.

- **The weight of all foods:** It will need to be calculated to determine the overall weight of the vehicle and its content, including passengers.

- **Space and storage needed:** What will you be losing in terms of space for other equipment, which could be important. Where you can store your food that will be the coolest part of your vehicle out of the sun.

- **How is it packed:** To keep it fresh and clean and to prevent lose and spillage?

- **Cooking time:** You will not want to be cooking all night long when you find a good camp. So, keep it simple and practical.

- **Ease of cooking**: Unless you have invited Gordon Ramsey along to prepare your meals and obviously swear at you then keep preparations and ideas to a minimum. You can be cooking easy simple quick and tasty meals with just a bit of imagination.

- **The cost:** It is not cheap to buy ration packs nowadays, costing an average of £4-6 per pack. You can keep cost down by hounding (in a good way of course) your local supermarket for their help. Also in many developing countries, eating out often is cheaper than buying in.

- **Food hygiene** It is extremely important that you do your best to avoid food poisoning or dysentery as this could prove to be a big inconvenience to you and your group. It is good practise to make list when preparing for an expedition and when it comes to hygiene, there should be no exception.

- **Plenty of soap and hand wipes:** Especially when preparing food, you need to wash your hands as prevention is better than cure. Hand wipes become an essential part of your kit and great for cleaning and disinfecting most things. You could even use them when no shower is available.

- **Keep fresh food wrapped up and air tight:** If you have containers then use them.

- **Gone off food:** It is better to dispose of out-of-date food, especially in hot countries.

- **Fly net:** When preparing a meal cover food that is left unattended with a fly net and away from the ground.

- **Equipment:** Keep all utensils and plates, cups, mess tins, pots, and pans clean. Use plenty of washing up liquid and clean thoroughly and rinse well.

- **Cooking:** Make sure the water is boiled and the food is cooked right through.

- **Eating out:** In many developing countries the water is not safe to drink, so be incredibly careful when ordering salads as they may have been washed in untreated water. The same goes for watermelons and ice cubes. Even plates that you are unsure of, then you should leave the last layer of food on.

- **Sharing:** Drinking out of the same water bottle or having a free for all at the cooking pot should be avoided as it could spread an infection throughout your vehicle. One person can be treated a whole team could be fatal. Instead, everyone needs their own drinking vessel and when serving food, the cook should dish out the food with the one utensil.

- **Safe water.** If anyone has done any survival courses at all, one of the first things you will learn is how to make water safe. It is common sense not to drink out of a dirty or stagnant body of water. If need be, then firstly filter it through a filter pump or straw or even some clothing. Then proceed to boil it. Purifying tablets are OK or even Silver or iodine. If you are in a hot country and there is no way of filtering or treating, you could build a still that would evaporate any kind of water even salt water. There are solar stills you can buy that would be more convenient.

There is a saying when overlanding. Make a list of the things you need but do not have and of the things that you have but don't need.

The next time you go travelling this list should start you off on the right foot.

What are your essentials?

Food and water are an essential life source, without which life is pretty bleak and not long living. It can be found everywhere with a few survival skills. It is not just the skill to be able to light a fire or know where to look for water that will save your life, but the desire and will to survive will also grow when this knowledge has been put to use.

You will find that you have become more resourceful as your will to survive is going to help you find more ways out of any sticky situation.

Having the right skills for the job in hand is always going to help and will give you the anticipation to see what could happen on your journey and how you can prepare and overcome any obstacle. The more you practise however the easier it will become for you to remain in a state of anticipation.

It never hurts to have that extra practise; it can only improve your chances of success.

Check, learn and use your equipment in simulated circumstances that you may face on your adventure.

Make sure you have a good grasp of the workings of any navigation system before you set off. Although they are not rocket science they can be very frustrating when you are not used to them and I'm sure that many broken screens and arm propelled launches out of a moving vehicle to be left to never navigate again has been the result of not having a good working grasp of a system before they are needed.

Before I buy any equipment that is an essential part of my kit, I look at reviews. I try to see it being used in videos even if it has been recommended to me by a friend. Who is to say that it will suit your ways and habits.

In the case of a backpack, it may not fit to your body the way it would to someone else's and therefore can become uncomfortable. You may like different compartments internally or it might just bug the hell out of you.

Buying online takes a lot away from the experience you will have with your product, but can be cheaper, so you would have to rely on reviews and feedback. If you would rather spend that bit more than do your own review. Check for comfort keeping in mind how long and how much you will be wearing it. Check also for ease of use and everything is where you like it to be.

You will want to check for quality, durability, and reliability. On any expedition or adventure that is testing, equipment is important, quality always cost less in the end. So, do not cheapskate and think logically and always improve your chances.

Possible Overland food list.

Canned Tuna

Canned Soup

Canned Black Beans

Canned Kidney Beans

Canned Chilli/Hearty Stew

Dried or fresh Fruit

Canned Whole Tomatoes

Canned Tomato Paste

Spices: Sugar, salt, pepper, Italian Seasoning, Garlic Salt

Olive Oil

Almond/Soy Milk

Energy Bars

Spaghetti Pasta

Spaghetti Sauce

Fusilloni Pasta

Nuts

Coffee

Peanut/Almond Butter

Small jar of jelly

Hot Chocolate

Hersey Bars

Marshmallows

Crackers

Saltine Crackers

Cold Cereal

Instant Oatmeal

Steak Sauce

Balsamic Vinegar

Sriracha Chilli Sauce

Cholula Hot Sauce

Tortillas

Chips - Salsa

Overland equipment Checklist

Water (2 gal. per person per day)

Cooler (cold foods according to your meal plan)

First Aid

Tent

Map/GPS/DeLorme

Clothes

Bedding (pads, sleeping bags, pillows)

Camp Kitchen

Table

Chairs

Coleman Lantern

Coleman Stove

Trash Bags

Propane

Insect Repellent

Camp Bowls

Silverware Sets

Wet wipes

GSI Pinnacle Camper Kit (pots, pans, plates, cups)

Thin Plastic Cutting Board

Coffee Filters & Pour Over Kit

MSR Water Filter

Fire Bag

(lots of ways to start a fire – wet, dry, strike, lighter, fuel, gels, etc.)

Cooking utensils

Knife X 2

Paper Towels

First Aid Kit

Bottle/Can Opener

Aluminium Foil

Napkins

Kleenex

Paper Plates

Toilet Paper

Folding Chairs (4)

Fishing Poles (3)

Dish Washing Station

Sleeping Pads

Vaseline

Clothing

The art of knowing what clothes to take with you on your epic and life changing adventure can be a headache at times, but it also can be enjoyable and exciting because you are imagining yourself living your travel.

Again, it all depends on where you are going and what time of the year.

During a time in South America, I was working as an overland tour driver where I would have to drive the circuit of the continent.

This meant that I would be driving through many different climates and attitudes.

This would present a conundrum when it comes to choosing what clothes to take with me.

You may have heard this before and have some knowledge of it and may know already that when temperatures drop you then add layers. It is all about layers. The more clothes you have on the warmer you will be as air gets trapped within layers. when the weather warms the layers come off. So, if you pack 2 items of each size from a vest to a thick jacket making up at least five layers. You should have enough clothes for all occasions and to see you through the wash days.

Buy at least two pair of quality cargo pants, which are particularly good and comfortable for working in. They also have plenty of carrying pockets.

But in reality, it is whatever you feel comfortable and practical in.

You will need at least two pairs of shorts. One pair to be able to swim in, and the other for all other occasions.

You will need at least ten pairs of socks if you do your washing once a week. I say ten because there will be times when your feet get wet or the days on long hikes and show a bit of respect for your teammates.

When it comes to footwear, I usually take with me a good comfortable pair of walking boots that are breathable and as waterproof as possible. Using Scotchgarde or any other useful product to weatherproof your boots and certain equipment you may feel needs it, will prolong its life, and help keep you dryer and more protected.

I would also buy them a few weeks before I start my travels just to wear them in and get them used to my feet. Blisters can be very painful and demoralising and could slow you down, preventing you from doing and seeing more and most of all could stop you enjoying the experience.

I also take with me a good comfortable pair of trainers. Which I would also wear in.

118

A pair of walking sandals and a pair of flip-flops for them beach times is a good idea as in very hot weather they become very welcome.

Vaccinations

Although vaccinations are not always needed, they should be taken. You can visit your GP and they will discuss with you what you need.

Malaria tablets are only needed in dense areas of forest where malaria is considerable risk. Dryer and high attitudes will be malaria free.

However, if you are travelling through dense jungle and high malaria risk areas then you should be taking the prescribed number of tablets and when they should be taken. You should think to yourself is it worth the risk and peace of mind. You could easily find what vaccinations you need, for what country and where to get them online.

Events

When planning your overland adventure keep in mind of any events that may be happening in wherever you're travelling through.

Make a note, set dates, and work it into your routes as part of your journey.

There will be times when you are travelling through small towns or villages or even from big cities where you come across an event that you may find interesting.

So, when you are planning your route take this into consideration and add more time at those places.

There will be times when you go to a place that you have been longing to go and it falls short of your expectations. You may have planned to have spent two or maybe three days there when one would have been plenty. You may want to cut down on this event and save it for any other that may show up on the horizon.

The Plan

When planning an overland expedition, you should always give yourself enough time. One year is still sometimes not always enough, but if you are dedicated you can do what you need to do and, in the time, allocated.

Below is a manageable to do list over the course of one year.

You can print this out and use it as a guide.

12 months to go.

- List potential team members.

- List what you expect from your team members, such as money, time, usefulness, and temperament.

- Contact potential team's members. once you have your members of your team you will want to get as many contact details from them as possible so that they are in easy reach.

- Arrange a meeting between members of your team and discuss, strengths and weaknesses.

- Discuss the Aims and goals, Destination, and changeable and achievable Routes into the time that coordinates with the person with the least time.

- Assign jobs to team members. It would also help if all team members could do a small part in the department, they are weakest at, which would not only help them improve at that subject but that also there's a better understanding of the planning and adventure throughout the team.

- Prepare risk assessment and information sheets.

- Discuss modes of transport and which vehicle would best suit the team and its purpose.

- **Preparing yourself,** Undoubtedly the most important part of any successful serious overland adventure is knowing yourself and realising the task you are putting before yourself and your team, and what you must do to combine you, your team and the task to be in harmony. Read and watch documentaries and ask others who have experience around your expedition.

- Suggest to each of your team members to purchase a copy of this book, so you are focusing on a closer wavelength with each other.

10-8 months to go.

- Make a list of kit, equipment, food, navigation tools, vehicle and money that you may need from sponsors if of course you want help funding your travels.

- Draw a plan on approaching and contacting potential sponsors, such as emails, setting up meetings, cold calling, and following up your last contact with your intended sponsor (Remember to be persistent, but not annoying).

- Start arranging any fundraising events you may have in mind. (Keep it simple but keep it fun).

There is much more about Sponsorship and fundraising later in this chapter.

8-4 months to go

- If your journey involves a vehicle that is not being sponsored, then start Searching for a vehicle that's suitable or of course unsuitable depending on the challenge that you have set.

- Start gaining some vehicle knowledge. It is best if you and another team member knows some basic vehicle maintenance and gain at least a little expedition driving knowledge as breaking down in a desert or other extreme environment can be a stressful situation, which could be avoided with some basic skills.

- This is the time to start buying and testing your kit and equipment.

- Go on mock weekends, firstly to test equipment and secondly to gain a stronger bond with team members and work out any indifferences.

4-1 months to go

- It is visa getting time. (Read the paragraph on visas and passports below)

- Start testing your vehicle within this time, as it will give you time to iron out any major problems, which could get worst on the journey.

- Make sure all vehicle documents are correct and in order. It can cause a lot of unnecessary time wasting.

- Check that your communication methods, i.e.: mobile, satellite equipment, laptops, sim cards etc are activated and ready to go.

- All the maps for your routes are studied and stored in a compartment solely dedicated for them. This will help to keep them in good condition and unlost.

- You will need to check all the items on your list throughout this month as it will be by far the busiest and stressful.

1 month to go

- In this month, it should be, check, check and recheck again There will be things that still need to be done and some which just turn up to try to put a last-minute stop on proceedings. But remain calm, focus on the goal, and get it done without hesitation.

- Your finances need to be sorted and in order. It is better practise to have control of any issues that could occur on your return. It has happened to me more than once, that my eagerness to travel has left me in a crisis on my return. But if you have that persistent attitude, it will not take too long to be back in the swing of things and certainly don't let that thought deter you from your dream's.

- By now you and your team will be at emotion central, but never panic, the cool head will always win through.

Leading up to your adventure, you should still be improving your mindset, your team's relationship, and the relationship with your sponsors.

Passports

Give yourself plenty of time for passport organising if any needs renewing, I would suggest at least two months before departing.

Also, have somewhere to store your passports. A safe fitted to your vehicle, or a hidden compartment.

You should have somewhere that you fill is safe on your person for keeping any valuables.

Visas

Visas are tricky as some countries will not process them until you are virtually ready to leave. Some also require letters of invitation. These can be obtained through in country travel bureau's, who for a fee will also arrange your visas.

Going to embassies is cheaper, but extremely time consuming.

When filling application forms it is best to be honest as refusal can bring delays.

Never rush them and always do what is asked. After you have rechecked for errors and if possible, ask someone else to check also. I had a Russian visa application returned to me five times; on the sixth time I had learnt a lesson.

Carrying luggage

Carrying and storage of your luggage for an overland expedition can prove to be one of the biggest headaches of the journey. If possible, create compartments for each team member, the messy culprit will stand out. Remember though as a team of leaders you are responsible for each other, and it would be of no use to go charging in with only the concern of part of the team, help them find a solution to improve and lead by example.

Keeping a vehicle tidy for weeks on end that is used by a group of adventure travellers is never going to be an easy task, especially when tiredness creeps in on the many long days and extremely rough endless dust tracks. Make time to sort and tidy the vehicle and your kit. This will save a lot of frustration when looking for much needed equipment in the dark.

I would certainly suggest that the spare wheels and fuel be kept on the outside. A good solid roof rack or door racks maybe suffice, but make sure the racks are bolted onto and through your vehicle as they will be put to the test and shaken to their core as the roads get rougher and less forgiving. The smell of fuel on the kit can be annoying and spills can damage important equipment. Spare wheels are too heavy, dirty, and cumbersome to keep moving around to find stuff.

Health and fitness.

"Health and Fitness is like a marriage; you can't cheat on it and expect it to work."

- Bonnie Pfiester

It is not necessary to be an Olympic athlete to participate in overland travel and most expeditions require no more than persistence and determination, which in itself can make you do extraordinary feats of endurance.

It is no secret to say that the training you put in to prepare for your challenge should more than match the expedition itself.

Your mental ability will show in the discipline you put in to the preparation for the journey.

The more you put in the more you will get out. This goes for every aspect of the planning from sponsorships to buying clothes.

Being in good health is vital to a successful expedition. Even if you suffer from asthma or are disabled in any way.

Eating correctly and training correctly, depending on the challenge before you, will give you the best chances both physically and mentally.

It will help improve your confidence in your ability to accomplish your goal.

It will grow your discipline to improve and achieve the task you put in front of yourself.

Chapter 4

Fundraising for your event

Whatever you want to achieve in life takes work. It takes dedication, it takes motivation and driven desire.

Sometimes to get what you want; you have to do what you don't want and most of all you need to persevere and be persistent at it.

It can be a chore and you will find yourself making excuses not to do it.

It has never been my favourite subject, but if funds are low and dreams are high it is a duty that must be fulfilled.

I am saying this from my perspective as there may be people out there who relish finding the funds that they need.

There are many ways of course you can raise funds, but before you start you need to write down your reason WHY!!

- Why are you setting out on this adventure? your goals?

- Why are you choosing this form of travel?

- Why do want to go where you are going?

- If you are raising money or awareness for a charity, ask yourself why? the sponsor will want to know.

Once you have written down and understood your reasons why, you then should write down for what it is you need sponsorship.

Not all sponsorship is for money. It maybe for the fact that you need a good satellite navigation system or spare parts for your vehicle or even a vehicle. It could be that you need to pay for classes that could help you gain the knowledge you may need.

Ask yourself questions such as:

- What it is that you need sponsoring for?

- Who are your likely sponsors to be?

- what you expect from them?

- What you are willing to give them in return?

You will now want to know how you are going to do this. Again, write it out and ask questions:

- How can I contact and find the person I need to talk to?

How can I make the offer I am putting to them sound so attractive that they will want to give you an offer you can't resist?

Keep asking questions until you are satisfied that you have the tools to seek sponsorship.

Prepare yourself!

Plan everything in detail and practise. Plan your approach to the sponsors you have chosen that are perfect for your adventure and that you are perfect for them, even if they do not think it yet.

Set out the way you want the funds raised to help you in your cause and stay focused.

134

Write out plans on how you are going to save or how you are going to raise the money. Do it with as much detail as possible as this will help it become more real and give you a better insight with more chance of attaining your fund-raising goals.

Saving

You can save by putting your hard-earned money away each week. This can be an arduous task and require more discipline than expected. When trying to organise an expedition you will always find things that will need paying and they always find ways for you to dip into your savings.

Look at giving up a luxury and put that money into a jar that you have no way of access until you leave.

Organising events

You can run a small event. These can be fun to set up and create an interest in what you want to achieve by those who attend your event.

You must use your imagination on this and see what inspires you as this could be endless. It could be something simple from a raffle to a full-scale sports day event.

Sometimes it would be better, depending on how confident you are in creating an event or you may think an events coordinator or organiser who could run and set it up for you better and raise more funds. They can be expensive but if they are good, they can bring in more money for you then you could yourself.

Putting out a plea

This could be anything from a small ad in a local newspaper to a big ad on a local radio station.

You would simply tell the listeners or readers about yourself, about your goals and simply ask if there is any way they can help you. It would be good if you could have a list of items or money that you may need.

Sponsors

The three sponsors that you would be looking for, would be the public, local small businesses and corporate.

When it comes to getting the public to sponsor you it would be best that you have a little more incentive for them. This could be in the way of having a limit of what you want to raise for yourself and your team and your needs to accomplish your challenge. The rest of the sponsor money will be going to a certain charity.

If this is so you will need to get permission from the charity and preferably ask if you can use their logo on your sponsor forms. They may even have sponsor forms that you could use and would save you a lot of effort.

This still can be quite demanding and can put people in an awkward situation when you ask them to sponsor you. So, I like to never hide the fact that I am going to ask for money from them. This prepares them and if they are interested when you say you are raising money for your overland expedition then you are more likely to get something and usually more than what you would have done if you did not prepare them.

I would start off with family and friends and work colleagues.

So, it would be worth having a few copies of your sponsor forms to pass out to family members or friends that could be in a position to get your sponsor form filled.

Small business sponsors

Getting a sponsor from a small business would be much simpler than getting it from a corporate sponsor. It may be a shop, a public house or even an online business. You could simply have shirts printed with their logo, tagline, and business address.

Quite often a small business may welcome the chance to have their business advertising this way, as it would show that they have a heart and a sense of value.

Corporate sponsors

This is a different kettle of fish. Corporations can be very demanding and quite literally not worth the hassle. But if they can cover all or virtually all of your whole adventure and possibly your vehicle and cost then that may be the way to go.

You will have to persevere with them and keep them happy by doing what they ask of you.

Usually, the day your expedition starts will not be the end of the task you have to do for your sponsors. Sometimes it may be that you have two call in to a radio station with announcements of your progress. Other times it may be updating them on their blog.

Asking for free stuff.

It can be well worth your time and effort and put your pride aside to ask if someone has something of use to you that you can have a no cost.

There are plenty of supermarkets that waste and throw food that could save you a small fortune and see you through your travels.

There may be even electrical companies that can help you with a sat-nav that maybe faulty and you feel you could fix it and make it work for you. You will have to use your imagination on this one, as there is a limitless number of ways to get free stuff. But it is definitely worth the time and effort and can be very rewarding both with what you can get and what you can learn from the experience.

Travelling for Charities

It is what you give in this world that counts and if you can do something for someone else for your trip the more fulfilling it will be.

It could also help you get much-needed support and attention.

There are so many charities that could use your help, so it is just a matter of who you would want to help and why.

There are community charities that help schools and communities in countries with less opportunities. There are many conservation charities that would love your help and awareness. Also, animal trust that could use your support.

Give it some thought with your team as it would give you a larger purpose and goal. It could help with easier passage through border controls and spot checks too.

Persistence

Be persistent with your goal at fund raising until you get what you want.

You will get a lot of no's but don't let that set you back just look at it a different way and see what you could have done better and then return. But whatever you do, do it in a way that is inspiring and not in a way that is annoying.

The best way to get anyone to do anything is to make them want to do it. So, give them reasons to want to sponsor you. Get them involve and ask them questions on what could be the best way to be productive for them. Make them feel their importance and they are part of the inspiration behind it.

Tell them that your respect for their business and its values are what has driven you to your decision of wanting them. At the end of the day, you want them to help you achieve your goal and if making them feel important to your adventure gets you what you want, everyone wins.

Chapter 5

Overland survival driving

On most occasions whilst driving through remote towns or villages you will stand out like a clown at a funeral. The locals will want to know who these strangers are and where are they from and why are they driving that monstrosity. You will get a profound sense of adventure as you stare back at them and their lives.

It can be awe-inspiring and difficult to imagine until you are there, and you are driving through some of the most amazing scenery the world has to offer.

When you are a team, you cannot wait until it is your turn to drive at least that was certainly the case with me. Being a professional driver of some of the biggest trucks on the road and taking them all around the world for almost 30 years, I relish the challenge and have a lot to say on the subject.

Some days can be extremely difficult and testing on your mind and in your heart. When everything seems to go wrong. When you are bogged down and seems like there is no way you are going to be able to dig your way out as your vehicle sinks even further into the deep sand or mud.

The sweat is dripping from your face as you dig frantically and the fear of being stranded in the harshness of a vast desert looms closer.

The harsh reality of overland driving is exactly what it says on the tin, it is overland. Meaning there are not always roads and sometimes not even tracks, where you will be creating your own paths to get you where you need to go. So, your team and you can have a pretty dreadful day if you are not prepared.

For instance, driving at high altitude can cause many difficulties to yourself and your team and of course your vehicle, as there will not be enough oxygen for you to breath or for your vehicle to burn.

The altitude will also cause water to expand which could lead to another host of problems in the coolant system.

Increasing your chances by planning and preparation for your journey can make for a much more enjoyable and successful completion of your expedition. As I have been saying all through this book about preparation and how important it is in all areas of your adventure. So, then preparation is key and should be never overlooked, it could mean the difference between life and death and usually it is a great exciting life if you succeed or a miserable tragic ending to a promising life if you fail and are under prepared.

Of course, however it is dependent on where you are planning to travel. Nowadays you are never far from help or a town in the middle of nowhere. It might still be a struggle, but the chances are on your side, and it can be a really good way to understand the culture of the local people and give them a chance to understand you.

But if your route takes you through barren and remote terrain that will test you and your vehicle to its limits, where you will not see another living soul for days or even weeks, I would highly recommend that you seek the required knowledge to help you prepare for any unlikely situation that could cause a tragic end.

In chapter 3 is the list of tools and equipment that would be required for a successful outcome.

On a negative note, you can guarantee the tools that you have will not fit a certain nut or bolt that is causing difficulty.

So, you must learn to adapt improvise and look what you have got and how it can be adapted and used sufficiently enough to get you out of trouble and back on your journey.

It is not enough just to have the right tools; you must at least be resourceful enough to learn how to use them and adapt them to your needs.

The wear and tear on your vehicle when driving overland can be a disaster if again you are not prepared to be able to fix it and of course do your best to prevent it. Prevention is better than cure after all.

I will begin now by offering you simple tips and advice on driving styles and habits that can make it or break it. Habits that are bad such as riding the clutch, driving and parking to close to the curbs and cutting in, which will explain about further in the chapter.

Using your gears correctly.

I am very guilty on this subject of taking inefficient vehicles with clutch problems on a road trip. However, it has always been through advanced countries where help is always at hand.

If your clutch does go and you find you can't get your vehicle into gear, it is not always the end of the world and there are certain techniques you could use to get out of a very sticky situation. If ever you find that your clutch pedal isn't having any effect on your gear changing, then usually your clutch as failed and gave up the ghost. So, stop the engine, put your handbrake on and then put the vehicle into second gear with your foot on the clutch.

You then let the hand brake off start the car and lift the clutch. This will cause the vehicle to jump into gear and start moving. Yes, you will only have one gear, but it could get you out of trouble and you could always although not pretty, crunch it into high gear as you pick up speed.

Riding the clutch is a terrific way to make sure you wear it as quickly as possible.

The clutch pedal should be pressed down and then straight into your selected gear change and then released as soon as possible, all the way up and foot off even as many car driving instructors will say to you as you approach a tight and slow bend to put it into second and keep your foot halfway down on the clutch pedal.

There is no need for this and will drive easily enough and safely enough around the bend with your foot completely off the pedal. It will also give your clutch a longer lifespan.

Changing up and down should be practised and timed listening to your vehicle's engine or of course if you have one watching the rev counter. You would want to keep it the lower part of the green as much as possible and when you are changing up into a higher gear you will be looking to be in the upper half of the green.

Sometimes when setting off driving on steep inclines and mountain passes it will require you to go out of the green. But you will not have to go far to get into the next gear.

You will hear me saying this a few times in this chapter, it is all about momentum. Whether you are driving through a big city or across a sandy desert you need momentum for a more enjoyable and less stressful drive.

Over revving your vehicle will cause unnecessary wear and tear on your clutch, gearbox and your engine, and will also start to cost you more in fuel. so, listen to your engine and watch the rev counter. Over revving on steep mountain passes will start to cook the engine. Keep watching your gages so your vehicle is running the best it can be.

Under revving could cause stalling and put your engine and gearbox in unnecessary stress. Always try to keep your rev counter in the green and practice listening to the engine as it will tell you how your driving is.

Snow and Ice

Driving in ice and snow can always be difficult and unpredictable. You will find that being an overland driver you will come across these many times. Even in countries that are closer to the equator have areas of high altitude and in winter months can have a lot of snow and ice, they can also be very unpredictable when it comes to weather and change will happen in a matter of minutes. This is where your preparation and awareness come into its own.

Of course, practice makes perfect and the more you do it the better you become and let us not forget safer.

When steering on slippery surfaces you do not want to pull on the wheel sharply, this will cause the momentum of your vehicle to continue in a straight line when you wanted to be turning. As you can imagine this can be extremely dangerous.

You will want to turn smoothly as if you are drawing a semi-circle whilst you are light on the steering and not jolty or heavy.

If you start off in first gear in heavy snow or thick ice on the road, you will just wheel spin and not get anywhere fast.

It is always best to start off in second or third depending on the gradient of the road. This will prevent wheel spin. As your vehicle starts moving and increasing in speed by using the clutch, change it into a higher gear as soon as you can. You will then keep a steady speed and using momentum to execute without too much revving as this will cause wheel spin which you would want to avoid at all costs as it will give you less control of your vehicle. Whatever you do you do not want to be breaking harshly, you will just skid and hit something. Use your gears to slow you down and ease of the momentum.

Mud and Sand

Mud and sand driving is a rule amongst itself. As like ice and snow is very unpredictable but in sand unlike ice, you are less likely to slide and skid into other vehicles or ditches. Although mud can be extremely slippery and very boggy in thick areas such as forest or fields.

If however, you do get stuck in mud or sand it is always a good idea to take sand ladders with you. They are heavy and cumbersome but can get you out of trouble and save your life.

On occasions when I have less room in the vehicle and need to lighten the load, I take with me a roll of carpet or an old rug. You don't want to be cutting out large chunks of the living rooms wall to wall fitted carpet or your wives favourite Persian rug that has been in the family for 6 generations, instead ask around through friends or anyone decorating their homes or go to a local carpet shop and ask if they have any cut offs they can spare.

Using the carpet under the stuck wheels will give it the necessary lift to get you unstuck and continue your journey. It is also a much cheaper option than using sand ladders.

Again, is all about momentum and keeping up a continual speed that will see you through the obstacles you face as once you do come to a halt is highly likely that you will be stuck there, so get your shovel ready and your sand ladders out.

There are many places you will drive through that are very boggy or sandy and likely to get stuck in. So, plan your run up and speed and stick to that speed without having to change gear, as by changing gear you will loss the necessary momentum to carry you through.

Acceleration

To point out the obvious accelerating is all about timing. You would never accelerate when you go around the bend or down a steep icy road. You will not want to be going up and down on the accelerator which would cost more fuel and Wear and tear on vehicle. Always keep it steady and gradual and once you start picking up speed be able to know that you don't have to take your foot off again until the next obstacle, be it a bend or traffic lights for instance.

You will want to be changing gear as your accelerator is revving, this will allow the gear change to much smoother and have less wear and tear on it.

Once you are going you will be looking and listening to your engine and rev counter, this takes practise, but is very worth the effort as you will learn more about your own driving style and the way your vehicle is performing.

Breaking

If you are using your gears and accelerator correctly and focus on the timing of your drive and obstacles you face, you will be in a position to use your brakes a lot less. This will not only save fuel because it will prevent over revving your vehicle as you keep having to pick up speed again. It will also save wear, tear on your brakes, and stop any brake fade, it would also mean that you are giving yourself, your passengers and your vehicle a much smoother and less stressful ride.

If you need to brake on ice or snow quite simply you are driving too fast. You should practice your driving skills and practice not using your brakes as much as possible, it will only cause you to skip and lose your control over your car.

You will want to slow down using your gears.

Aquaplaning

Have you ever heard of the saying **aquaplaning**? If you are driving too fast and you come to a large puddle in the road and decide to use your brakes to slow down it will cause your wheels to lock and act like skis. This will cause you to lose control and the vehicle will have a mind of its own.

When approaching a puddle even if you do not see it until it is too late, and you are going through it, do not break! It is better to use your accelerator to keep your wheels going around and preventing aquaplaning. If, however there are vehicles in front of you, firstly if you need to hit your brakes you are driving too close and should ease off anyway and if the inevitable should happen it is better to use the puddle to slow you down and ease down with it by pumping the brakes. When you pump the brakes, you will prevent the wheels from locking up and be able to keep control.

There are going to be times you will come across extremely steep hills that can go on for miles and miles when you are travelling overland. This can be a problem if you are heavy for on your brakes. You will need to drive in a lower gear but keep the revs with in the upper green of the rev counter.

You will want to pump the brakes slightly and enough to slow you down. If you do keep your foot on the brake, you are very likely to overheat the brakes, that can cause brake fade or even complete brake failure and possibly cause them to catch alight.

Pumping the brakes every for few seconds will allow the brakes to slightly cool and help prevent a disastrous situation.

Many vehicles now have ABS, which is the abbreviation of advanced braking system. This will allow the brakes to be pressed continually as it is designed to pump the brakes many times over in a short space of time. This will give you much more control over your vehicle, but still do not do this constantly and learn to use the brakes as little as possible and let them cool down as much as you can. You will not only be driving smoother and safer, but you will also prolong your breaks.

Coasting

Coasting is where you simply come to a hill and when it is safe to do so, take your vehicle out of gear and just let it roll down the hill.

I know however in many countries it is illegal because the less control you have over the speed of your vehicle. The benefits of coasting are saving fuel and of course less wear and tear on your engine.

For instance, if you are travelling through a very mountainous area and you are going downhill, it is possible you could coast for 2, 3 or even ten miles. Doing this on multiple occasions especially if you are travelling for many weeks could actually save you a small fortune. However, you must always be aware of what is in front of you and use your timing correctly. If of course you need to put it back into gear, then select the highest gear or that of what is relevant to your speed.

Steering

It is without a doubt the most important part of driving. If even for a split second you do not concentrate on your steering, you can end up down a ditch.

It is important to know that this could happen when you are travelling overland as road conditions are not always up to the standard you may be used to.

If your steering is correct and under control, then you can usually get out of most situations safely.

A controlled skid is purposely putting yourself into a skid situation and being able to get out of it. An out-of-control skid is when you hit black ice or any other obstacle that causes your vehicle to move out of control. When the rear wheels start to come around in front of you it is best to always turn the steering into the direction of the skid. This will help to prevent the vehicle from a full spin and eventually right itself.

It is not only your speed that gives your vehicle and your passengers a smooth ride, but also the way you steer and how smooth your control is.

Bumping over curbs with your back wheel because you have taken the turn to sharply can-do damage to your tyres and suspension over time. Just remember to steer wide enough to allow your rear wheels to not hit or scrape the curbs.

When you are going around bends on the winding country road or steep mountain pass, you should be looking at the traffic ahead for any obstructions and keep your car as evenly curved as possible on the bends and try to meet that bend at its apex when you drive into it and leave the bend as early as possible to keep the vehicle more in a even curved line and less sharp turning.

There is a driving style I call cutting in. I am not too confident that this is a very much used term, but it does exactly what it says.

Cutting in is when you are driving around a bend and instead of taking the bend smoothly and as fluid as possible to give a smooth ride, you take the bend on as if it's got a sharp pointed corner. Meaning you jolt the steering at its sharpest point causing the vehicle to turn quicker than needed.

The tyres instead of smoothly going around on one level using the whole surface of the tyre, is then put under stress, and lent over to the side with the whole weight of the vehicle on the edge of the tyre causing it to cut in to the road. This is not only bad for the tyres over a long run, but if you are in a van or truck, you will find that any luggage or other compartments with your kit and equipment in will come flying out at you from all angles.

To get a little philosophical driving is always smoother and better for all involved when you are driving is in a flowing motion. See it as the wind hitting a building. The wind will not hit the building take a short step to right and then move straight forward again. It simply flows around in a swirl.

This all helps with the momentum of your driving and enjoyment for yourself and your passengers.

If you are wound up and angry over something, then until you calm down let someone else drive.

Maintenance

Just 10 min a day or a least every second day, do some walk around checks on your vehicle.

This will not only get you to know your vehicle but also give you an heads up of anything that could or has gone wrong, so you can put it right as quickly as it happens.

The daily check should consist of:

- Battery. You want to check that the terminals are not loose, and all the wires are connected and not exposed. That the battery is safely stored and bolted down so it can't come loose. Make sure it is in good condition such as check for leaks and that it is topped up with distilled water. I will also personally on long journeys grease the terminals.

- Check all your fluid levels. Check the oil level is topped up to the full mark on the dipstick and that it is not too black as it may need an oil change or there is no water in it producing a brownish white creamy substance.

- Check also there are no oil leaks. If there is a puddle of oil underneath the engine in the morning, chances are you have an oil leak. You will want to check out where this is coming from before it could cause a bigger problem.

- Water is topped up and check if there is any oily substance in there by rubbing it between your fingers. if possible, add antifreeze with the water this prolongs the life of the water system.

- Check that there are no water leaks. Checking the radiator all pipes and around the water pump seal.

- You will want to look over all electrical components underneath the bonnet, for instance the Alternator has all the wires firmly placed into it and are not exposed or worn. Constant vibrations can cause wires to start to come loose. Most of the time it can be just an annoyance but the other time when you least want it, it could cause your real problem.

- Go around the vehicle checking the tyres are fully inflated and not torn or worn excess. Driving over rough roads will shred tyres and give no mercy to your vehicle.

   Check all your lights work and change them as soon as possible if there are any faults. As you may never

know what will happen when driving through countries with truly diverse whether conditions.

- Check the windows are not cracked and the windscreen wipers are working and in good condition.

- Check the steering is not loose and wheels are straight. You could have easily gone over a rock or down a pothole that could have put your steering out of line. This will also wear the tyres out at a much faster rate.

- Make sure the brakes are good and solid and that you have confidence in them to stop you in an emergency. You will more than likely whilst on your travels get from time-to-time dust and grit in the brake linings. Most of the time this can be blown out or brushed off.

Getting stuck

If you do manage to get stuck in sand or mud and even snow, deflate your tyres a little so they spread wider over the ground giving you more traction, could actually be important enough to save you and your team from a bad situation.

There have been cases where people have gotten stuck in the desert sand and died because they did not have any basic knowledge that could have saved their life.

You of course will have with you your sand ladders or sand mats or even an old rug that should get you out of trouble. There are however many other ways that could get you out of a situation and a terrifying experience.

The image below shows of a technique that is simplicity in itself but can be very effective.

It simply involves tying a stick or a prank to your tyre that can hold the weight and then you just start driving.

You will need to tie it with strong rope through the wheel itself.

Winches

If you are using a winch, then you will need an anchor point. If

you are in the desert this is not always going to be possible.

But using your sand ladders as an anchor to attach your cable to, can be a highly effective way of getting yourself out of very deep sand, quicksand or even a swamp.

You simply dig a hole deep enough to drop your sand ladder into by about two or three feet. Then you will want to dig a groove into the sand or mud for the cable to reach and attach to the sand ladder or any other strong flat and wide surface.

If you do not have any sand ladders or there is nothing that you could use or that is laying on the ground that you can simply improvise and use as a solid base to pull yourself out.

You have however and should have at least two spare tyres and wheels. You should use at least two wheels with two separate ropes that attach to your winch cable.

Once you have done this you simply fill in the hole around your sand ladder or tyres and start your winch.

This has the effect of pulling against all of the solid ground, making a very solid anchor point. See the two diagrams below of these examples.

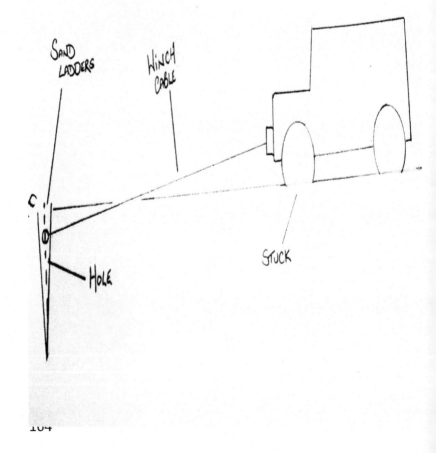

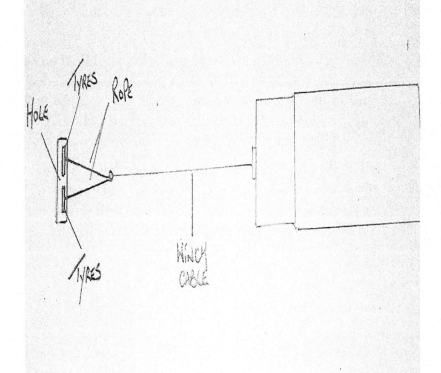

There are of course many places you can put an anchor point, such as trees, post, and even other vehicles. It is all about improvising.

Sometimes it is worth going overboard with whatever method you use. Meaning, for another example, you are being towed out by another vehicle, use two ropes instead of one, if of course you have a spare. You will be putting less strain on both and have security that you will be pulled out from an unpleasant situation.

If you use one rope it will have to take the full strain. If your vehicle is routed right down it could take double or even triple the weight of the vehicle. If your one and only rope breaks or gets badly weaken, it will create a nervy drive until you can purchase a new rope.

If you do only have one tow rope, you should double it up in effect making it twice as strong. This does make the length much shorter for the vehicle pulling you out, and this may not be possible but it's better than having no rope as you may be able to improvise.

Chapter 6

Surviving continents

.

In this chapter I will be explaining and giving valuable tips and ideas for surviving and getting through with as little hassle as possible, the continents you may be driving on, on your overland adventures.

Starting in alphabetical order of the continents that I personally have required knowledge and experience in driving through.

Africa

Africa is a very vast and diverse continent and made up of fifty-one countries on the mainland.

There are also many different and remarkably interesting cultures that make Africa an intriguing and exciting continent to drive through.

Tour companies are big business in Africa mainly because of the reputation that precedes this continent. People use tour companies to go overland here because of safety issues.

Of course, we know of the corruption and poverty that rule these lands and you should be prepared and aware of the possible dangers. However, wherever you go on this planet you should always take with you your optimism. You should always look for the good and you will find it and it will find you.

When driving through Africa you will come across many difficulties as well as much beauty and diversity.

You will not always find the greatest of roads, nor will you always find the best luxury hotels to rest your weary head. You will more than likely be Bush camping or staying in run down so-called hotels that have poor plumbing, electric cables hanging out of every wall and a bed with more stains than a butcher's apron. But of course, this is Africa and as soon as you get used to the idea that is how it is out there the better it will be.

This continent holds something special in my heart and I love to travel through this wonderful place. It offers so much and every day there is always something weird and something wonderful that could and does happen.

It seems that everyone is a mechanic and that if in the unlikely event of your vehicle breaking down you can find somewhere and someone that will fix it for you, but for a price of course. However, no matter how much these prices you are charged, it will always be way cheaper than anywhere in the West.

As time goes on whilst on your overland travels and of course the more you do you will begin to master the art of bodging, meaning you will fix any problem with whatever you find. It will always be a quick fix and to get you out of trouble and to your destination. Africans are great at this, and they have a whole history of making the most of what they have and making it last.

I personally like to take a bag load of football shirts with me when I am travelling there. The excitement for them in a football shirt of an English club will get them to do anything for you.

Also, what they lack is toys for their children and of course learning materials. They also need medicines, so another good idea would be to take painkillers, you can buy them very cheap here and will be very much appreciated.

There are many patrols stops, I would say every 20 to 30 miles. This is where the fiche form comes into play and will make life much easier and less stressful for you and your team. Also, the best chance of any corruption between officials and yourself from not happening.

Border crossings are a stressful enough place on their own and in Africa they are like a trading post, where locals will try to sell anything and everything to those crossing the border. If you are a Westerner, you are a prime target as a potential customer.

Border officials not always but will be looking for a bribe.

Even if it may take two or three hours longer you should never bow down to bribes because in Africa there will be many and once you give them what they want they will be looking for it from the next unsuspected travellers. They are only asking you because of the last set of over Lander's paying them a bribe.

You must always keep a cool head at borders and not just on your journey. Expect and anticipate that anything can happen at any time.

In 2011 my vehicle broke down between the Mauritania and Senegal border. It was obvious to the locals we had broken down as we had to push our Jeep into Senegal.

Virtually instantaneously we were surrounded by the best Jeep mechanics in all of Senegal.

To save any bad atmosphere I let them help me fix my Jeep of which it was running very well afterwards and gave them a football shirt. When they stop smiling and thanking us, we went on our way.

Fuel, be aware!

You will need some way of filtering your fuel because it would not always be clean.

When travelling vast miles and fuel stops are few and far between. You will need to carry fuel containers or Jerry cans. Sometimes they may have filters on them and if not find a way to filter the fuel, even if you use a whole sock.

You will want to make sure it is what you asked for, and you are not being ripped off.

Petrol is much finer and less oily than diesel. Diesel is very oily and dense which is why it is much harder to catch alight. Before you go you should get used to the different smells as they are both very distinctive.

Some of the roads in Africa are car killers, you can quite literally here your nuts and bolts on your vehicle being shaken loose. As said in an earlier chapter you will need to re-tighten your wheels and suspension and check on a regular basis. You will come across many washboard roads; this is where sand and dust have hardened like concrete and created many long narrow hard strips that run the width of the road just like a washboard or sometimes called corrugated roads.

These roads will shake you to the bone and they are responsible for breaking more suspensions than any other type of road.

The one kind of suspension you do not want to be driving on across corrugated roads are leaf spring suspensions. They are just too hard and not enough play or give. You will end up crawling over a washboard road just to stop you bouncing out of your seat.

With coil springs you will have the option of driving over them at a faster pace which will help you practically glide over. The slower you go the bumpier it feels.

Security

In any situation you will want to stay safe and protect your belongings. If possible, have at least a boot/trunk to stash your kit and equipment. I know this is not always possible but at least do your best to either make a storage compartment a secure hidden place and never leave your valuables on display.

I personally made the mistake and of course learned from it when I took a vehicle that had a soft top and transparent plastic windows, a clear temptation for opportunist. It was always a worry if we had to leave it out of our sight. It is never worth the hassle that you could get from this. So, make your vehicle as secure as possible.

Have good hiding places in your vehicle that you know are well hidden and you trust will not be found, so you can stash any money you do not want to carry with you in less safe areas.

Asia

This is a great continent made up of many different and diverse countries, cultures, languages, and religions.

It has some of the best driving routes in the world from the silk Road to the Himalayan passes.

Asia truly has many contrasting cultures, from the central Asia of the old Soviet Union where a sternness of the lands of no smiles is not always the greatest of welcomes, to the absolute over friendliness of the Japanese or Iranians.

Here there are huge mountain ranges and vast deserts that will evaluate you and your car to a point of destruction.

There are plenty of washboard roads and a lot of the time, there are any roads at all.

This continent is also extremely diverse in the cost of an expedition. For instance, if you are travelling through Iran you will need to have a carnet De passage. This is your passport for the car to tell them your car is roadworthy, and you will not be leaving it for them to pick up the pieces. A carnet De passage is extremely expensive and can be up to £1600 for your vehicle. However, once you are in Iran fuel works out to be around £0.20 per litre. In fact, living expenses are cheaper than staying in a tent. You won't have gone far to find accommodation that is less expensive than paying for a campsite.

It isn't until you drive through China where you can find it is expensive in some areas and cities and particularly the cost of being granted access to drive through the country. Food and fuel are cheap and so is accommodation. But to gain entry requires a lot of work and money. Including your visas, your vehicle registration and a guide who would have to come with you and be paid by you and anything else the border crossing wants to charge you.

Europe

Driving Europe is a relatively easy thing to do nowadays. With good roads and good places to stay it is not really a hardship. There are also many different countries and some interesting cultures. There are lots to see and do and with so much history and scenery to take in.

Fuel stops are plentiful, and you will always come across one, so you can never make excuses that there are no fuels stops if you run out.

Driving through the European continent is also easier and the fact that there are no border crossings any more makes it a breeze.

There are plenty of campsites and good hotels with decent food and combined with a good navigation system you will barely break a sweat at any time.

All this is great but if you have not got enough money to buy a royal yacht you are going to struggle. Everywhere is expensive and following the trend, anywhere a tourist goes the prices are high.

However, it is possible to travel through Europe on a shoestring. You should look for cheap campsites or if possible do as much wild camping as you can. Be aware, some countries it is not allowed, but if you start looking before it gets to late in the day and dark, you may find an out of the way field to pitch a tent.

Shop at supermarkets and street markets for food and accessories and try not to eat out unless your wallet is too heavy to carry.

There are lot of toll roads. If you are in a hurry, these are the quickest options. There are also plenty of free routes and if you add these to you planning and schedule then there should be time to save on tolls.

North America

North America is a wonderful continent to drive around. It has many terrains and climates, from deserts and mountains, salt pans and beautiful coast to high-rise cities and many places of interest.

As you can imagine you are never far away from getting out of trouble. However, there are still some vast landscapes that could prove a test for any survival expert. So always prepared for the unexpected.

You could actually drive from one side of the country to the other without seeing anything other than main highways. Of course, you are an adventurer and like me want to see as much as possible. So, driving on back roads and through small towns and cities that barely exist on a map are plentiful here. There are many places you will have to get to via track roads and usually when you get there it has been worth the valiant effort.

Never in the states be afraid to ask for help because they are only too happy to give you the shirt off their backs.

176

It is an absolute blessing after struggling with pidgin Spanish and Arabic to be able to converse in your own language, even if they say I'm the one with the accent.

It does mean that by being able to speak the same language in sorts, it was easier to get about and more helpful if you go down the wrong track and get lost.

Now in the states it isn't always possible to find anyone to ask, because it does in many states seem that no one walks anywhere and it's home of course to the gas guzzler, which makes it very handy that the fuel is cheap here.

The east is the cheapest around $1.75 to $2.20 per gallon, compared to $2.90 to $4.50 in the west. If you need fuel, it is always best to fill up way before you actually need to. Because when you need it you will not be able to find cheap fuel, but only when you fill up you find the cheaper station just around the corner and the difference between one gas station and one next door could be even more than a dollar.

The fuel will be good and should not cause any trouble to your engine. But you will still need to take a spare fuel filter just in case of dirt and dust getting into the fuel system.

It can be expensive to travel the states and comes down to your budget. Campsites are plentiful but gets remarkably busy in the summer months. Even in the middle of nowhere you will find a campsite. These places usually have limited facilities, and the toilets are often in bad condition and where many large spiders and snakes make home.

If cooking whilst camping, be sure to clear your mess and put food away securely or at a distance from your camp, as bears will be attracted by your presence.

South America

As a continent South America is made up of many cultures that you can put into two or three categories. Very Christian, carefree and an attitude of, that will do.

However, they are friendly and will put themselves out to help you. Finding a good mechanic could be a problem, so you will need to brush up on your mechanic skills before you leave. You will always come across the odd police checkpoint, and these can be quite corrupt if you give them the chance.

It is best to hold your nerve and make them wait, rather than give in to whatever bribe they are after.

Depending on the length of your journey and what countries you have decided to drive through, you will probably be crossing the Andes on many occasions.

Going back to the chapter on breaking you will be ascending and descending plenty of times, so much so you should have mastered it by the time you go home.

You will find that when you need parts for your vehicle whatever town you are in you should remember that they are built into sections, moreover they will have vehicle parts and labour all down one street and food or grocery down another. This is a thing I found throughout the continent. So, if you do need anything for your car is best to find out where this one place is before you leave and put it into your notes.

Going back to the mentality of this continent it really does show when they are behind the wheel. Regardless of the size of the vehicle from a car to a truck or even a bus full of people, they will overtake even on the tightest bend on the highest mountains. Some towns can be absolute chaos but unlike the West there is very little road rage, even in places such as Peru where the horn is used 100 times more than the indicators.

There are some extremely high roads and very high cities. Attitude sickness will get to you in your first two days of your visit.

Drink plenty of water, no alcohol and get some sleep. Once you get used to the altitude you should be okay. Usually with me in my first few weeks I still feel the lack of oxygen and have to take a deep breath every now and again.

When we struggle to breathe, so too do our vehicles. They need oxygen to burn and if they do not have enough, it can cause the engine to stall. There is not much you can do on this subject other than keep your time at high attitudes to a short a period as possible. Of course, sometimes this is not possible but when you are planning this, you could look at ways this can be reduced. Taking Altimeter with you is a promising idea.

At high altitudes water expands and could cause problems in the water system. Before you go to high attitude reduce the amount of water in the water system, so when it expenses it has somewhere to go without causing any damage.

Currency in South America changes from country to country and is usually not worth the paper it's written on. There are plenty of ATMs spread throughout and most of them are free to use.

I have never drove through one country in South America where it was not a self-service fuel station. There was always someone there to fill up for you. Maybe it was just job creation. Fuel is relatively good and whereas in central Asia diesel is extremely hard to get hold of in some countries, which is not the case in here. However, still use a fuel filter and take a spare fuel filter in your tool kit and if you can, keep your tools organised and easy to get to.

All said and done driving overland is about planning, preparation, and most of all a positive, optimistic attitude. Whichever continent you travel, learn from it and flow with it. Experience as much as you can.

Conclusion

The end of the book could be the beginning of your greatest adventure.

-The Author

What you get out of life is what you put in. So, seek inspiration and imagine.

Having read this book, you are in a place where you have an understanding and knowledge of WHY, WHAT and HOW, to create an adventure for yourself.

However, it is not always possible to keep you motivated with words from a book. Unless that book is followed religiously.

The word motivation is made up of two words with two meanings.

182

The later Latin word – motivere or motivus which makes up the first part – motiv, meaning to move or a more literal meaning is **a reason to move.** Now translated into English as motive.

The action part of the word is to take action.

Motivation = A reason to move, to take action.

There are two reasons why people take life changing actions.

The first is inspiration. Using inspiration is fine, but to keep you motivated, you need to be inspired on a regular basis.

The other reason is the complete opposite to inspiration but could get you to reach your goal in a much faster time. Therefore, desperation can be a much more powerful reason to get motivated. It comes with sentences, such as, I must do this before I'm too old or while I am still young enough.

Find your inspiration or even your desperation.

Let it drive you to imagine, plan, prepare, live, and reflect on your life's greatest adventure.

Thank you for reading. I hope your journeys are great ones.

Happy trails

Acknowledgements

As I am writing these acknowledgements, I cannot help but to feel overwhelmed by the people I have shared these experiences with.

Almost every detail of this book comes from my own learning and living experiences, giving me the opportunities to explore and write about what I am most passionate on.

However, without fellow travellers and explorers to watch, travel and make friends with this would have been an impossible task.

So, I would like to give a huge thank you to all those friends I have journeyed with and met along the many paths.

I have said within this book about what inspires you and what are your values and goals.

This paragraph is dedicated to my mum, Rose. Who supports me and always helps when it is possible. She is always there if needed and, on many occasions, after long times away travelling and returning with no money to pay for a bus, has given me a roof over my weary head, until I've have gotten back on my feet and stable enough to travel again.

Lastly to anyone who gets inspired by this book or any other means of inspiration, which allows them to experience overland travel and what it can do to grow and excel their life and passion for adventure.

Printed in Great Britain
by Amazon

45042335R00106